HELMING AND YACHT HANDLING

HELMING AND YACHT HANDLING

Stuart Quarrie

Helmsman Books

First published in 1996 by
The Crowood Press Ltd
Ramsbury, Marlborough
Wiltshire SN8 2HR

British Library Cataloguing in Publication Data

A catalogue record for this book is available from the British Library.

ISBN 1 85223 943 3

Picture Credits
All photographs by Stuart Quarrie
All line-drawings by Terry Johns

Typeset by MultiMedia Works Ltd, Gloucester
Printed and bound by BPC Books Limited, Aylesbury

CONTENTS

*I*NTRODUCTION

This book is written with the aim of giving assistance to anyone who has ever had a problem either coming in and out of harbour or getting the best out of their yacht at sea. As well as one section on general helming at sea, there are sections on handling in harbour under both power and sail, with detailed analyses of most berthing and mooring situations. The manoeuvres include all those needed to cover any of the RYA cruising syllabi up to and including Yachtmaster Offshore.

Equally useful to both cruising and racing sailors, all manoeuvres are described with the aid of simple-to-follow diagrams and cover everything from simple, everyday situations to the more esoteric types of manoeuvre. Although written from the point of view of handling a sailing yacht under sail and power, the sections on handling under power apply just as much to single screw, displacement motor cruisers.

The author has been involved in sailing and the teaching of sailing most of his life and has been a Royal Yachting Association cruising instructor for over twenty years. He has experience in the techniques needed in virtually any situation and on board most types of yacht.

KEY TO DIAGRAMS

Most diagrams indicate wind and tide considerations, as well as movements of the boat. Use the following key when interpreting diagrams:

direction of wind

direction of tide

movement of boat

PRINCIPLES OF YACHT HANDLING

1

Whether under sail or power, it is vital that you understand the forces which are going to act upon your yacht before you get into a situation where a lack of thought could leave you in a difficult or embarrassing position.

All manoeuvres need to be carried out in the knowledge that if anything goes wrong, you have an escape route already planned out. It is not very sensible to take a yacht of any size, but particularly a large one, into a potentially difficult or dangerous situation knowing that one mistake can result in damage. Anyone who does this needs to rethink their attitude to skippering.

Unfortunately, given the pace of modern life, there will be times when one is forced into such a situation, normally by pressures of time. If this does happen it is still important to understand the dangers and to have considered any options which might be available in order to minimize the risks.

In most tidal mooring or berthing

This is a particularly well laid out marina, but even so there is little room for manoeuvring.

situations it is likely that the tidal stream will be the dominant feature and this means that nearly all mooring and similar manoeuvres will, if possible, be carried out against the tidal stream. Sailing against the current has the advantage that for a given speed over the land, the speed through the water will be greater and therefore control of your yacht will be that much easier.

Most modern yachts will respond well to their rudder even with as little as half a knot of steerage way. Thus, if you have half a knot of current against you, steerage way can be maintained even when stationary compared to the land. Conversely, if forced for one reason or another to approach a berthing situation downtide, you will need to be making considerable speed over the ground just to maintain steerage way and this obviously complicates the manoeuvre and can make it dangerous or impossible to achieve.

PRINCIPLES UNDER SAIL

When coming to or leaving a mooring or berth under sail, it is important that the basic working principles of the yacht are clearly understood. This is particularly important in the typical situation of sailing under reduced canvas, since then the normal characteristics of the yacht may be significantly changed.

The yacht will always pivot around the keel and to a lesser extent around her rudder, these being the two main areas of lateral resistance which are in the water.

Leeway

All yachts make leeway. Modern yachts with high-aspect, low surface area keels make very little leeway when travelling at full speed but the effectiveness of such a keel declines sharply as the boat speed reduces. So at the low speeds necessary for safe manoeuvring in

crowded marinas and the like, a yacht with this type of keel is likely to make much more leeway than normal. More traditional yachts with relatively large keels still make more leeway at slow speeds but the effect is not nearly as marked. This effect must be taken into account when manoeuvring at slow speeds, especially in strong winds.

Sails

Most yachts have balanced rigs when proceeding under full sail. However, taking a sloop as an example, once one of the sails has been furled, the yacht will become unbalanced, showing more weather helm than normal if just the mainsail is being used and tending alarmingly towards lee helm if only the headsail is drawing.

At slow speeds the apparent wind angle at which you will be able to sail effectively will increase quite significantly. This is due to the lack of headwind caused by the yacht's movement to draw the apparent wind forward. With only one sail working, there will obviously be no slot effect and this further reduces the efficiency of the rig.

If only the mainsail is being used, it must be realized that it is very easy to oversheet the sail, stalling it in the process and consequently stopping the boat. Both the leech tension created by the mainsheet and the position of the boom if you have a traveller need to be slacker than usual. If you try to sail very close to the wind with only the mainsail up, and sheet in hard with the boom on the centre line in order to achieve this, all that will happen is the mainsail will stall, the yacht will slow right down and eventually you will lose control.

Tacking with just a mainsail is usually possible but only if the boat has enough momentum before going into the tack. Remember that after the tack, the boat speed will be even less than it was beforehand and leeway will be correspondingly greater. Often

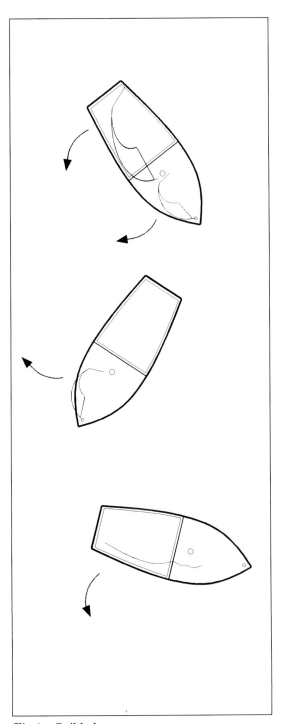

Fig 1   Sail balance.

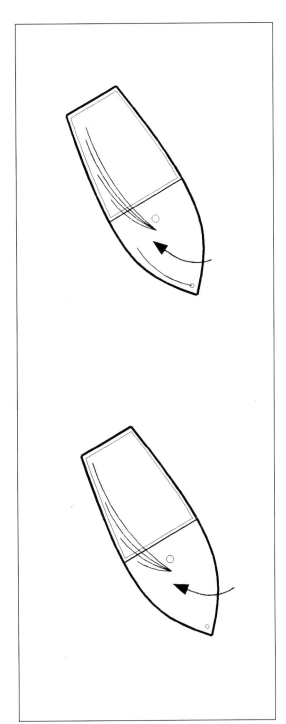

Fig 2   No slot – ease mainsail.

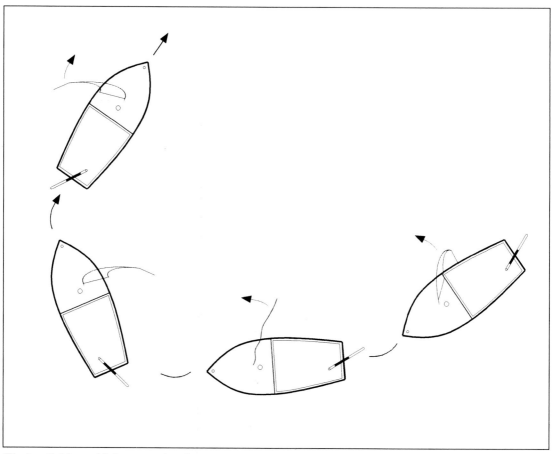

Fig 3   Gybing with just a mainsail set.

the yacht will sag to leeward by up to a boat length before she has enough forward speed to get the keel working again. Even if the yacht is relatively efficient, it will be even more important than usual to sail free immediately after the tack until speed has built up sufficiently to get the keel working again.

Gybing with just a mainsail is often very difficult and is bound to take a lot more turning room than normal. Remember that not only must the mainsail be let right out as you bear away but also that the yacht will pick up speed as it turns downwind. If you have misjudged the available space then this could result in a nasty accident. In some situations it

may be necessary to loosen off the kicking strap before or while trying to bear away. This will allow the sail to twist more and will reduce the weather helm, enabling you to bear away somewhat more easily.

If trying to slow right down with the mainsail set, consider the effect of the kicking strap. In most cases, even with the sheet eased right out, the back of the sail will continue to provide driving power unless the leech is allowed to flap by releasing the kicking strap. Scandalizing the main by lifting the boom with a topping lift is one good way to totally de-power the sail, for example just after a mooring has been picked up but before the

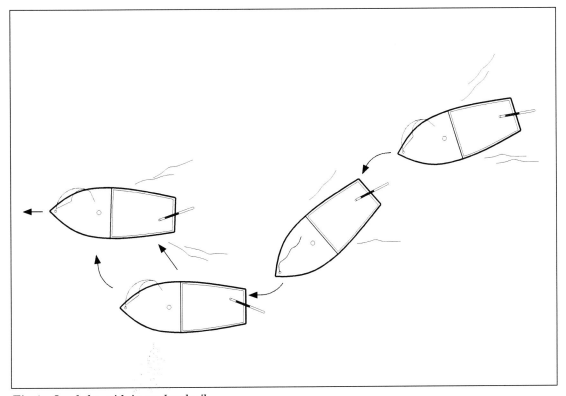

Fig 4   Lee helm with just a headsail.

crew have had time to drop the sail. Fully battened mainsails are even harder to de-power. Because they cannot flap they tend to be full and drawing all the time, if you push the sail out more then it just fills 'backwards'.

Sailing with only the headsail has its own drawbacks and problems. Because all the driving power will now be at the front of the yacht, she will inevitably generate lee helm. Tacking will be either tricky or impossible depending on the handling characteristics of the yacht. If you do tack, the yacht's bow will pay off considerably immediately after the tack until the yacht has enough speed to give good steerage-way. Similarly, if you have slowed down in your approach and now wish to speed up a little, as the headsail is sheeted home, the bow will tend to pay off, at least initially.

Mooring

In general terms, it is best to approach a mooring situation with the mainsail set if you know that you are going to be heading into the wind and that, once the mooring has been picked up or the boat is alongside, the mainsail will definitely flap. In these situations it is possible to use both sails and in light winds this may be the best option.

If there is a lot of wind it is nearly always preferable to use just the mainsail. This will not only reduce the amount of crew needed to handle the sails and reduce the speed of the yacht to sensible proportions, but will also make the yacht significantly quieter (no flapping headsail) and make the foredeck a lot safer.

If it is a wind against tide situation or for

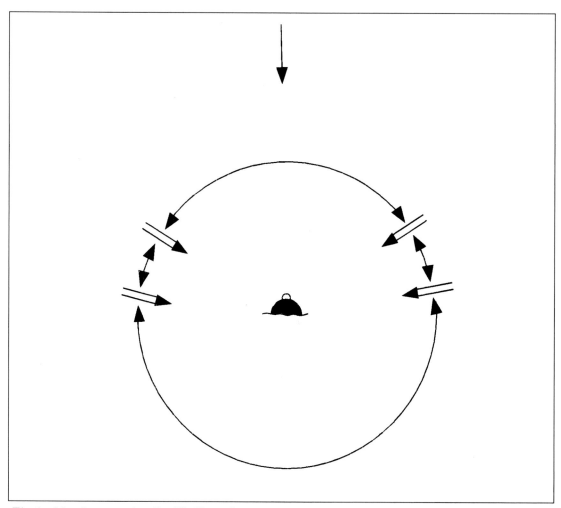

Fig 5   Moorings – mainsail will/will not flap.

some other reason you are forced to approach the berth or mooring with the wind either behind or even on the beam, then only the headsail should be employed. Some skippers advocate using the mainsail even in these situations and then being ready to drop the main the instant you have picked up the mooring. In my experience, while this approach can work it is fraught with dangers. Inevitably, this is the one time when the main halyard jams or something else prevents your crew from doing the necessary instant drop.

Under headsail alone you will be somewhat limited in your approach options since going upwind will be very difficult. This means that you must arrange to drop the mainsail in such a position that the mooring can be approached from upwind or at least on a reach. Having the headsail up will inevitably make the task of the foredeck crew that bit harder since the sail will be flapping around their ears.

In stronger winds it is often best to progressively drop even the headsail as the mooring is approached. Adjusting the amount of sail to achieve the required boat speed is a far more elegant option than letting the sail flap since you will end up on the mooring with no sails set at all and no flapping or hassle for the foredeck crew. However, this will only work if the mooring is being approached on either a run or very broad reach since, if the wind is on or near the beam, you are going to need drive right up to the mooring. Having a furling headsail makes this situation easier since the sail can be progressively furled as the mooring is approached, ending up once more with no sail at all as the mooring is picked up.

Another general point to consider is that of when and how to practise mooring or berthing under sail. Certainly it should not be left until the engine has broken down, otherwise you will find yourself under more stress than is either necessary or desirable. I like to practise sailing up to moorings and marinas on days when it is relatively easy and when there are safe 'bale out' options. Having the engine

ticking over in neutral provides the ultimate safety net.

In such practices do not be afraid to either bale out early or to use the engine if you have made a mistake or even if you are just unsure of yourself. It is far less embarrassing to do this than to hit another yacht or go aground in front of the watching 'experts' that always seem to materialize on such occasions.

PRINCIPLES UNDER POWER

Under power the yacht will have some of the same characteristics that it has when sailing but there are some significant differences. One of the most obvious of these is the fact that, in most circumstances, you can use reverse gear to slow down or stop. I say in most circumstances because if you come to rely on reverse then there will inevitably come a time when the engine either stalls as you go into

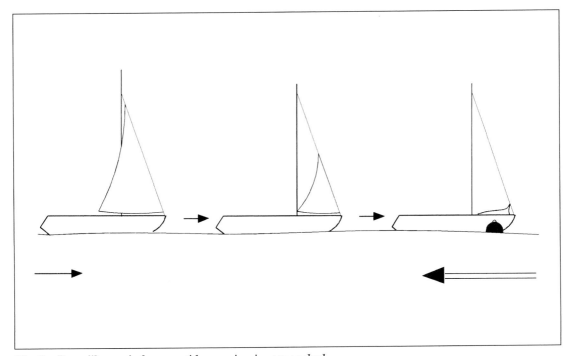

Fig 6   Drop jib as wind versus tide mooring is approached.

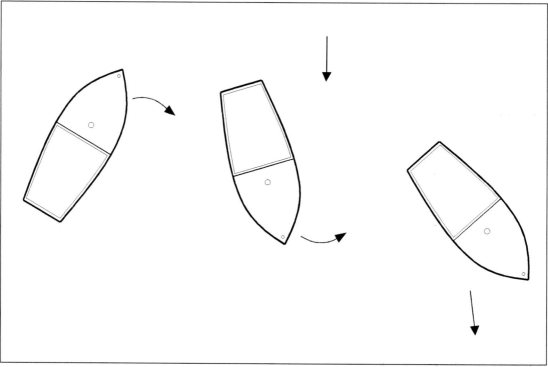

Fig 7   A natural angle to the wind.

reverse or for some other reason it is impossible to get into reverse gear.

With no sails set, any yacht will have a natural angle to the wind at which she will settle if left for a few minutes. With a single masted yacht this will nearly always be a broadish reach position. This is because in most yachts the mast and rigging, which comprise by far the biggest area of windage, are going to be set at or near the front of the keel. A ketch or yawl, with more rigging near the stern, is likely to settle naturally onto a beam reach or thereabouts The exact angle will depend on the relative positions of rig and keel and the sizes of the mizzen and mainmasts.

When manoeuvring a yacht for the first time it is worth while getting into an area of clear water and putting her into neutral with the rudder amidships to see how she lies. This data can then be used later when you need to be able to predict how she will respond in tight situations.

The Keel

The length of the keel will also affect how the yacht handles under power. A long keel will give straight line stability, ideal for long-distance passage making where you do not want a yacht which constantly twitches off course. The undesirable side effect of this straight line stability is that the same yacht will be relatively hard to turn in tight situations and will tend to have a large turning circle.

A yacht with a high-aspect, short chord length keel, such as a modern racing boat, will be twitchy at sea, going off course if the helm is let go for an instant. However, she will turn readily in harbour and is likely to have a very small turning circle pivoting directly around the short keel.

Because there are conflicting needs at sea and in harbour, most modern cruiser/racers compromise to some extent with keels that are neither ridiculously short in chord length, nor too long.

The Rudder

How powerful the rudder is will depend on a number of factors. One of the most important of these so far as low-speed manoeuvring is concerned is the distance between the keel and rudder. If the rudder is hung well back from the keel then it will tend to impart more turning force than if it is close to or even attached to the keel. A rudder which is balanced and free hung from the stock will be more effective than one which has a skeg in front of it. Similarly, the least effective rudder will be one hung on the trailing edge of the keel. In general terms, the safer and stronger the basic installation is for use at sea, the less effective it will prove for manoeuvring!

The Propeller

There are a number of types of propeller. Two or three-bladed, fixed, folding or feathering are all options which you may come across on different yachts and all give slightly different responses. For motoring, a three-bladed propeller is always going to be more efficient than a two-bladed one. However the downside is the huge amount of drag that a three-bladed propeller exerts while you are sailing. Folding propellers, often with small, inefficient blades

A Folder racing two-bladed propeller.

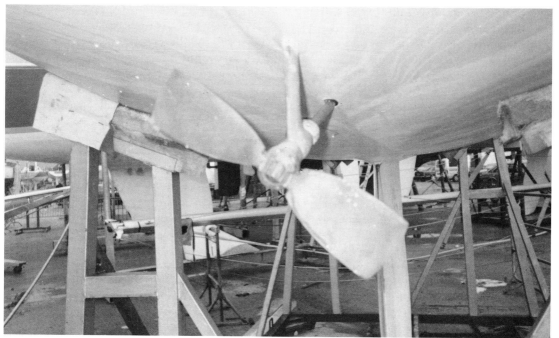

A two-bladed propeller with linked blades open.

A three-bladed feathering propeller.

give little driving force but correspondingly little drag when sailing.

Most yachts nowadays compromise with a two-bladed propeller, often folding but with reasonable sized blades. Some installations on racing yachts have a folding propeller with the two blades free of each other. This means that if one blade is sticky for some reason, it might not throw out when the engine is put into gear giving a characteristic unbalanced banging noise from the shaft. If you have an installation like this and it seems that only one blade has thrown out, then putting the engine into reverse normally cures the problem. Once the reluctant blade is out it will probably stay put with no further problem. However, most folding propellers now have the blades linked by a toothed gear which means that it is impossible for one blade to fold or unfold without the other one following suit.

The position of the propeller in relation to both the rudder and the keel will also affect its efficiency. To give a really good forward turning circle, the propeller should thrust its water flow onto the leading edge of the rudder. Thus, the rudder will be operating in fast-flowing water even if the yacht is travelling at slow speeds. If the yacht is fitted with a saildrive unit it is likely that the propeller will be some way forward of the rudder, reducing the effectiveness of the rudder at low speeds.

Manoeuvring

Propellers are called left or right-handed depending on their direction of rotation when in forward gear. It is important to find out whether you have a left- or right-handed propeller because this will have a profound effect on your manoeuvring, particularly in reverse.

In simple terms, the bottom part of the propeller works more efficiently than the top because it is in clearer water, further away from the hull of the yacht. This means that if

the propeller is, right-handed and rotates clockwise in forward gear there will be a small tendency for the yacht to steer automatically to the left. This occurs because the bottom of the propeller sweeps water to port and thus pushes the stern to starboard. The effect is small when going ahead because, with the rudder positioned behind the propeller, the water flow from the propeller tends to be straightened as it passes the rudder.

In reverse the effect is often much more marked. Here, with the same right-handed installation, the bottom part of the propeller will thrust water to starboard when it rotates anticlockwise. This in turn pushes the stern of the yacht to port. Because the propeller installation is almost certainly going to be in front of the rudder there is nothing to stop this sideways thrust. The yacht is turned, often quite significantly, by the propeller thrust.

This propeller wash, or 'walk' as it is sometimes called, can be used to great effect when manoeuvring so long as you make the yacht and its installation work for you. However, if you try to go against the direction of the effect then the yacht will be vastly more difficult to manoeuvre. Some yachts will be affected a lot by prop-walk and will simply not turn against it, while others seem to show very little difference between turning one way or the other – get to know your yacht!

If stepping on board a yacht for the first time then there are several ways to find out which way the yacht is going to walk in astern. If it is possible to see the propeller shaft down below then you can just put the engine gently into reverse gear while tied up and see which way it turns – anticlockwise when facing forwards means that it will walk to port and vice versa.

Often it is either not possible or at least not easy to gain access to the shaft. In this case the easiest way to decide how the yacht will respond is once again to put the engine into reverse while securely tied up, but this time to

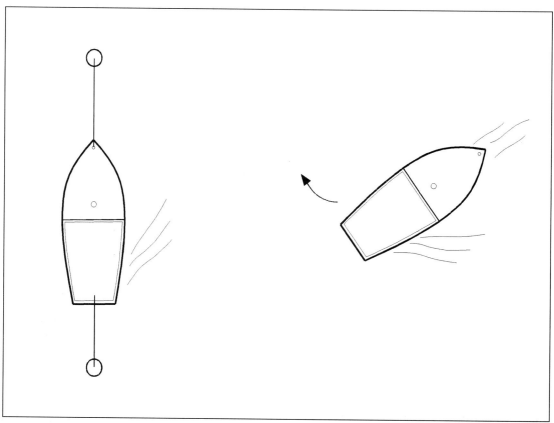

Fig 8   Determining prop-walk.

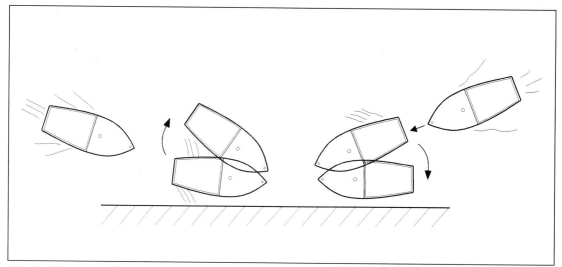

Fig 9   Use prop-walk coming alongside.

look over the side to see which side of the yacht has a flow of water coming away from it.

The right-handed propeller, which walks the stern to port in astern gear, will have a flow of water from the propeller coming out of the starboard side of the boat. A left-handed installation will have the flow from the propeller coming away on the port side.

If you do have significant prop-walk then always consider it when coming alongside or turning in restricted areas. With a right-handed propeller it will be easiest to come alongside if the pontoon is to port because as you put the yacht into reverse to stop, the stern will swing in towards the berth.

With a similar right-handed installation it will be safest and simplest to turn to starboard in any situation where you need to do a three-point turn. In this case you can commence your turn forwards with the rudder hard over to starboard and then, before you get too close to whatever the obstruction is ahead, go into astern gear, leaving the rudder over to starboard.

As the propeller goes into reverse, the prop-walk will swing the stern to port, thus continuing the boat around in its starboard turn. Only put the helm over the other way if and when you actually gain speed astern — otherwise leave the helm where it was and as

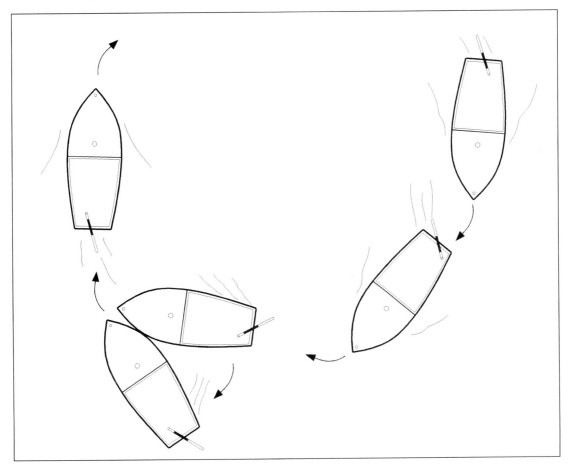

Fig 10   Use prop-walk in a three-point turn.

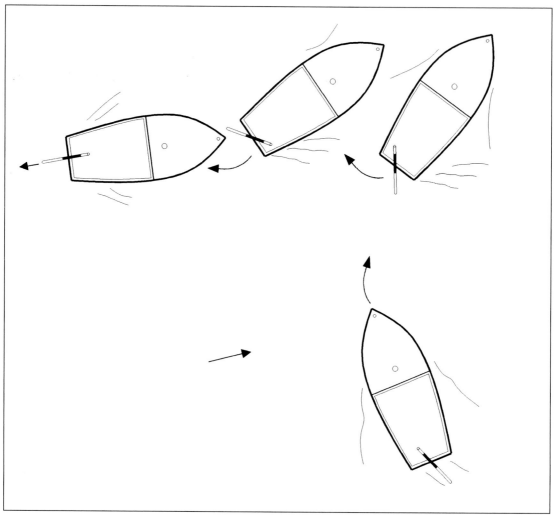

Fig 11 Use prop-walk to steer astern.

the yacht stops going forward give her another kick in ahead to continue the turn.

In open water, the combination of the natural tendency of most yachts to fall off onto a broad reach together with the prop-walk means that if you try to reverse into a space it will be easiest to do this if reversing into the wind. Get the yacht onto a broad reach position, with the wind on her port quarter if you have a right-handed propeller, then go astern. The prop-walk will swing her so that the stern is virtually straight into the wind and most yachts will go backwards quite happily like this. Once you have reasonable sternway on, the rudder will start to work properly (albeit backwards) and you should be able to steer more or less where you want to go.

One thing to be careful of in astern is the force of water on the rudder. Virtually all rudders will trail in a straight line when going

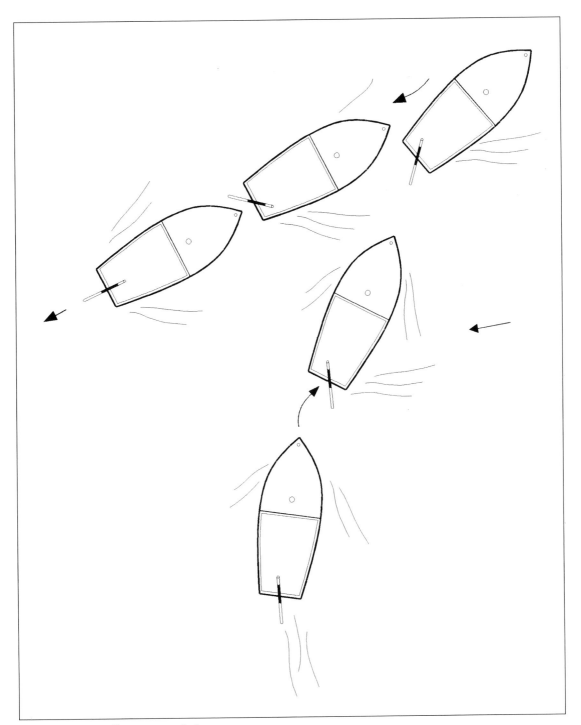

Fig 12   Prop-walk counters windage.

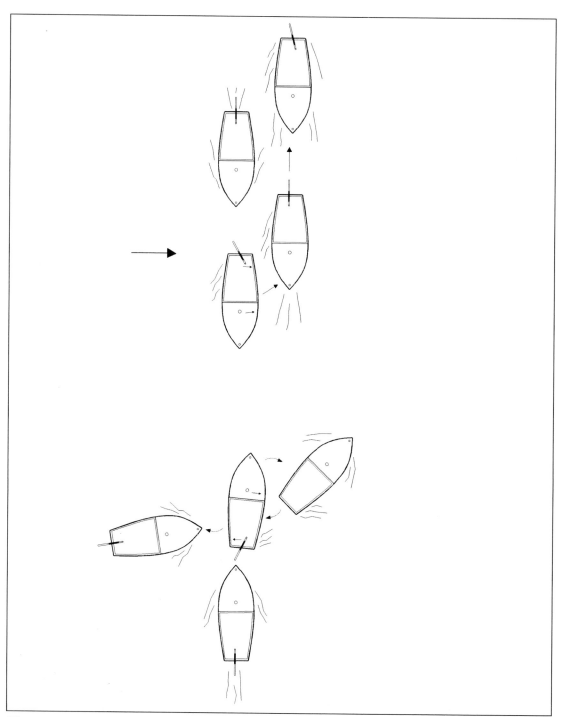

Fig 13   *Reversing with wind on the beam.*

ahead because the rudder stock (even on a balanced rudder) will be well ahead of the centre of the rudder. In astern the reverse is true and the force of the water going past the rudder is almost bound to try to swing the rudder hard over to one side or the other.

When manoeuvring astern hold the wheel or tiller tightly and keep your speed down to sensible low levels if at all possible. If you do accidentally let go of the helm, there is a real danger that the forces involved will swing the rudder over onto its stops so violently that damage may occur. Also, if you let go for a moment and then try to grab the helm again as it is swinging, you can hurt yourself quite badly – I once had two broken fingers from doing just that!

If you have to start your sternboard while facing into the wind, remember that as soon as you lose forward momentum the bow will almost certainly try to pay off downwind. If you are heading straight into the wind when you go into reverse, the prop-walk will swing the stern and it will be hard to stop her paying right off to a broad reach.

If you do need to go astern downwind, it is important to place the yacht so that the wind is going to counteract the prop-walk until you have gained sternway for steerage. In this case have the wind on the starboard bow with a right-handed propeller before going into reverse.

Reversing with the wind on the beam will be easy on one tack and virtually impossible on the other, depending again on which way the propeller turns. Going astern with the wind on the starboard side will be easy with a right-handed propeller and vice versa with a left-handed installation.

It must be remembered that with the wind on the beam, the yacht will make definite leeway, especially while going slowly and this must be taken into account in positioning the yacht before attempting to go astern. In anything approaching a strong wind, trying to

go astern with the wind on the other beam will almost always result in the yacht bearing off to a broad reach as the wind blows the bow off and the propeller kicks the stern up to windward. As before, it may be possible to steer properly once real sternway has built up but this will assume a fair amount of sea room.

PRINCIPLES OF ROPEWORK

It is important that the basic principles of ropework are understood early on in a skipper's career. While there is no right or wrong way of tying a yacht to a mooring or berth, there are definitely good and bad ways and these will change according to the situation. We will look in detail at some methods of tying up while looking at individual berthing and

This rope is being used for two jobs, which immediately makes adjusting more difficult.

An example of mooring with breasts and springs.

mooring situations later in the book. This short section just considers some of the basics which need to be understood and applied.

First we shall look at the functions of the different ropes that are required when tying up.

Breast Ropes

If tying alongside either a pontoon, quay or another yacht, the breast ropes are those going more or less straight across from your bow and stern to cleats or bollards on whatever you are tying to. Their purpose is to stop your yacht from yawing around so that it is no longer parallel with the pontoon.

These are almost always the shortest ropes used in tying up but they should not be made too tight, otherwise they are likely to snatch and possibly cause damage as the yacht rocks gently. Certainly tight breast ropes are a sure way of keeping light sleepers awake at night as

This yacht is moored alongside with breasts and springs.

they tend to make the yacht jerk unhappily. However, they do need to be tight enough to do their job and therefore a sensible compromise is needed.

Springs (1)

When actually tied up, springs are the ropes running along the fore and aft line of the yacht. Normally there will be one from the stern leading ashore to be attached near the bow of the yacht and a further spring running

Attachment of springs.

from the bow backwards and to be attached on shore near the stern.

The purpose of springs is to stop the yacht from shifting up and down along the pontoon. Because they are long ropes they will normally have a fair amount of 'give' in them and, because the yacht can pitch without affecting their tightness, they can be made much tighter than can breast ropes without fear of damage or snatching.

Springs can be run either from the ends of the yacht and back along the yacht side or from amidships. In general, the longer a spring is, the less it will need attention and the better it will work.

Springs (2)

Springs are used for a different purpose when leaving an alongside berth. If you need to force one end of the yacht to point away from the berth before being able to slip, for example if the wind is blowing you onto the berth or if there is another boat moored close to you in the direction you wish to leave, then the technique to apply is known as 'springing off'.

For example, if you want to leave in astern but need the stern of the yacht to be pointing well out from the berth, you would use a bow spring. This would be attached to a cleat at the bow of the boat and lead to a cleat ashore further aft. When leaving all other ropes should be released so that as you motor forward against this bow spring it is pulled tight. As it goes tight it will force the bow of the yacht in towards the berth, and at the same time the stern will gradually go out.

Initially it is just the natural curve of the yacht which forces the bow in, but eventually the bow is held rigidly by the spring, against a suitably placed fender. The yacht then pivots around the bow as more power is applied through the propeller. Once the stern is pointing out far enough, the engine is put into reverse and as soon as the load comes off the

Note the central attachment for springs.

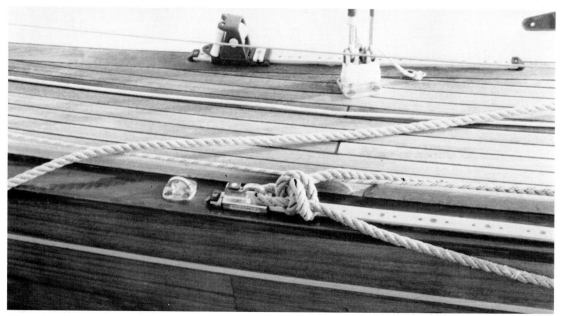

If no cleat is available then strong and secure deck fittings can be used instead.

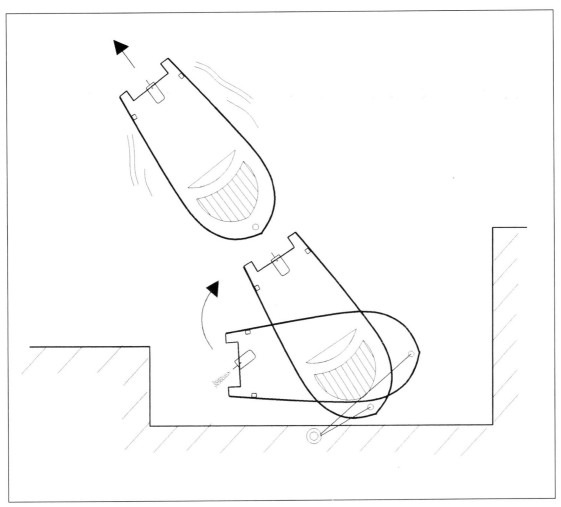

Fig 14   Springs.

spring it is slipped. You are then free to go backwards. Obviously the same technique can be used to spring the bow out, using a stern spring.

Head and Stern Ropes

These are warps going from the bow to a point on the shore further ahead than the yacht and from the stern to a point further astern. In a lot of respects they are similar to breast ropes but do not hold the bow and stern so rigidly in

place. Because they are by definition longer than breast ropes they can be tighter without fear of snatching. They also work to some extent to help the springs stop the yacht from moving along the berth.

If mooring to a floating pontoon, a compromise between true head and stern ropes and true breast ropes is often used. If mooring alongside a quay, where the tide is going to make the yacht rise and fall, then longer head and stern ropes mean that they will need much less tending than tight breast ropes. Here, it is

Stern line tied to a cleat but still permitting adjustment of existing moorings.

Mooring using separate breast and head/stern lines.

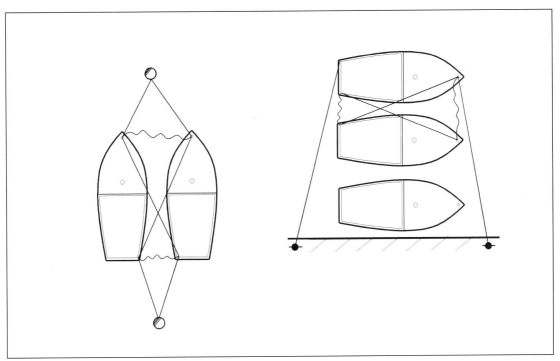

Fig 15   Shore lines.

Double lines are useful in case of bad weather.

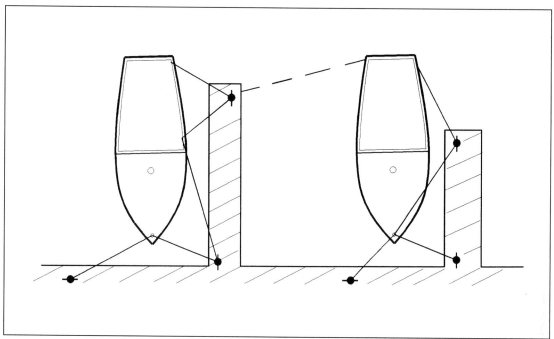

Fig 16   Second bow line.

A second bow line to keep her parallel.

usual to have relatively tight head and stern ropes and springs, together with loose breast ropes.

If moored alongside another yacht, on piles, or on fore and aft moorings then it is usual and polite to have breasts and springs to the other yacht plus head and stern ropes to the piles (or buoys). Similarly, if moored to a quay or pontoon on the outside of another yacht, it is courteous to have head and stern ropes going to the shore as well as breasts and springs to the inside yacht.

This courtesy is for two reasons. Firstly, if the other yacht wishes to move away from the berth, she is able to do so without first having to find additional warps to tie your yacht to the berth. Secondly, if the wind and/or current is strong, your lines hold you in place without exerting pressure on her lines.

If berthing in a marina on a finger berth, especially if the pontoon is a bit shorter than the overall length of the yacht, it is very worthwhile taking an additional bow line from the side opposite the pontoon to a mooring along the walkway. Between them, the two bow lines will hold the bows totally steady. If the pontoon is very short, which is a common enough situation in mainland Europe, it may even be worth taking a second stern line as well in order to stop the yacht from sheering around as the wind or tide changes.

Slip-Ropes

A slip-rope is one which is taken from your yacht, around a fastening ashore (or to the pontoon) and then back onto your yacht so that it can be slipped (released) from on

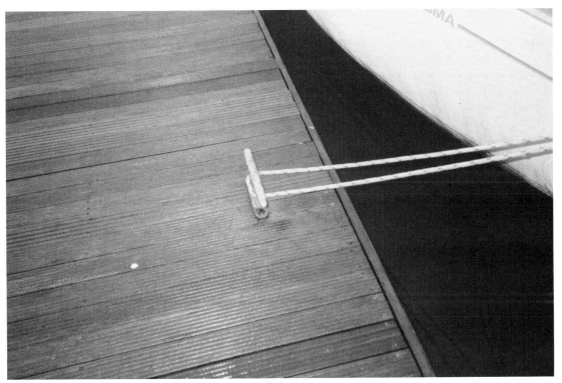

A rope rigged as a slip rope.

board. Unless only mooring for a short time the yacht should rarely if ever be left tied up with slip-ropes. These should only be rigged, if necessary, just before leaving the berth. This is because slip-ropes are more susceptible to chafe than any other. Also, when a warp used as a slip-rope does chafe, it does so in the middle of its length thus rendering the whole rope useless.

If tying up for any length of time, the end of the rope should be made fast, preferably ashore; the rope should then be tensioned as appropriate before being made fast onto a suitable cleat or strong point on the yacht.

I say that the end should be made fast ashore, rather than on board, as is commonly done. This is for two reasons. Firstly, if that particular rope needs to be adjusted, there is no need to leave the yacht to tend it. Secondly, even a neatly coiled warp lying on the pontoon

or shore is quite likely to be kicked into the water by mistake or even to be cut off and stolen!

I like to use a separate warp for each job if at all possible since once again this makes the tending of each warp much easier. If you do need to use one rope for two jobs then each end should be on shore with the bight of slack rope on board between the two cleats. However even if you take one end ashore, cleat the middle of the rope off on board and then take the rest of the rope ashore for a second purpose, it becomes impossible to make any adjustments at all to the first rope you tied and this can be a real nuisance.

Which Knot?

Some skippers have very fixed views on how mooring lines should be attached to cleats,

It is better to take the slack on board.

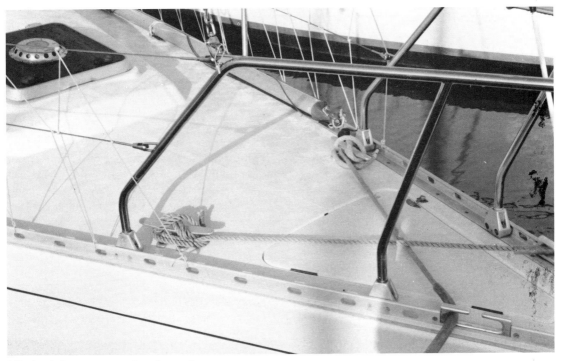

Nicely tied, a separate cleat for each rope.

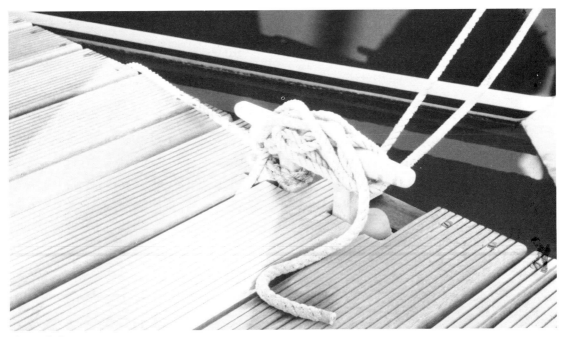

A tangled mess.

Sequence for adding your rope to a bollard. Prepare your mooring rope with loop and secure knot. Bring it under the existing rope and loop loosely over the bollard. Take up the slack but allow easy access for adjustment of the other rope, without the need to disturb yours.

bollards and the like, often with no real idea of why a particular type of knot or hitch should be used. Once again, in my opinion, there are no real right or wrong ways, there are merely good and bad ways and as before these will alter with each situation.

If tying the end of a rope onto a ring, bollard or cleat then the first thing to do in almost all situations, except for short-term slip-ropes, is to pass the rope right around the object twice (that is, a 'round turn'). The reason for this is primarily to reduce chafe as much as possible but also to allow the rope to be held under load while a knot is tied.

If a rope is tied, say to a ring, with a single turn, then as the yacht moves and the pull on the rope changes angle, so the rope will move around on the ring, causing chafe. If on the other hand a round turn is used, then as the yacht moves, the friction caused by the round turn will limit the amount that the rope moves on the ring, thus significantly reducing chafe.

The type of fixing used depends on many factors. If the rope is being attached to a ring or bollard then the two most common knots in use are the bowline and the round turn and two half hitches. (Note that even the bowline is actually preceded by a round turn.)

A bowline has the advantage that because the knot itself is positioned away from the ring, several ropes can be tied to the same object without the knots all getting jammed up together. The disadvantage of the bowline is that it can neither be tied nor untied under load whereas this is easy with the round turn and two half hitches.

Incidentally, if tying to a bollard to which another yacht is already tied, it is polite to attach your line so that hers can be removed without first untying yours. If the original rope

Round turn and bowline on a cleat.

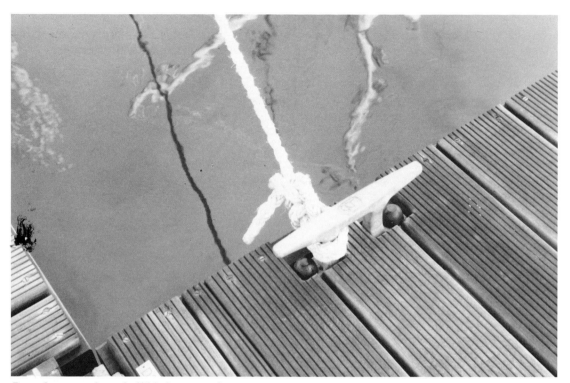

Round turn and two half hitches on a cleat.

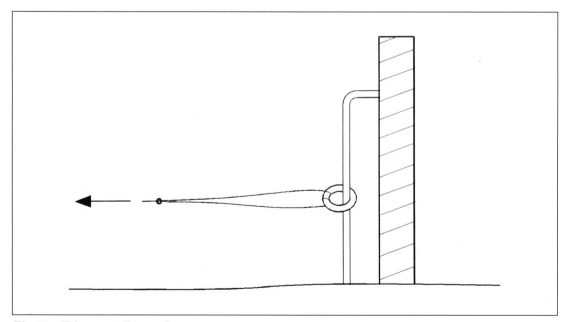

Fig 17   Tying to a pile mooring.

is tied onto a bollard with a round turn and two half hitches, then your rope should simply be tied underneath the original. However, if the original line is attached with a bowline, then it makes your life easier to pass the end of your rope up through the loop of the original bowline and then tie your bowline on top of the original rope. This allows either rope to be slipped without the need to untie either knot.

On a typical cleat, the end of the rope can either be made up with a round turn followed by at least a couple of figures of eight around the cleat, or once again a bowline can be used. If dealing with the end of a rope, I would usually use a round turn and a bowline here. If taking the middle of a rope onto a cleat I would use the figures of eight.

Tying to a typical pile mooring, there will be a steel riser with a heavy steel ring sliding up and down on it. Although for very short-term mooring, it is acceptable to tie your lines directly to the riser, for anything longer you should always attach your lines to the ring.

I would suggest that for this you should always, without exception, use a round turn and a bowline, with a longer than normal loop in the bowline. This allows you to untie the warp without needing to get too close to the pile and still allows the knot to be untied even if the tide has come in so far that the ring is under water.

If leaving your yacht alongside the same pontoon or on the same mooring for a long

Permanent mooring lines.

period, it is well worth making up a 'permanent' set of mooring lines. These can either be of heavy rope or a combination of lengths of rope (or flexible wire rope) with suitable splices and hard eyes to reduce to a minimum chafe with the warps shackled onto the shore attachment. If using rope in the system this should ideally be made of nylon since this will have the best stretch properties and will give rather than snatch.

2

YACHT HANDLING AT SEA

STEERING

Some people find the art of steering a yacht in the open sea comes naturally to them; while others find it really hard work, even after considerable practice. I have long been convinced that the majority of this latter group simply do not understand the principles of what they are trying to achieve – after all, the basics of steering are not that complicated.

If steering with a wheel the yacht will usually turn the way the wheel is turned, in exactly the same way as driving a car. As you turn the wheel it turns the rudder which deflects the flow of water off to one side. It is this which makes the yacht turn.

It therefore stands to reason that unless there is water flowing past the rudder, turning the wheel will have no effect – analogous to turning the steering wheel of a car while stationary.

If steering with a tiller, this might cause problems for the first few minutes because the tiller is attached directly to the rudder. If you want the yacht to turn to the left, you have to push the end of the tiller to the right and vice versa for turning to starboard.

However, most people get the hang of this after a very short space of time and many actually find tiller steering easier than wheel

steering for the simple reason that it is so direct.

Steering in astern is not hard but does take a little practice. Now, rather than the water flowing past the rudder pushing the back of the boat into a turn, the rudder is effectively pointing at the direction you want to go. Obviously all tiller or wheel movements will need to be in reverse.

One of the biggest problems which beginners have to contend with is the delay which often occurs between putting the helm over and the yacht actually turning. This response time will vary from boat to boat and will alter at different speeds, with a quicker response normally expected at fast speeds. It will also change depending on the load being carried on the yacht especially if the sails are not trimmed to keep the boat balanced as you alter course.

At very low speeds, with little flow past the rudder, steering will be imprecise and soggy. As the speed increases towards 'hull speed', the steering will feel much more precise and solid. Finally when the yacht is thundering along in big waves, the forces of wind and wave on the hull may become greater than the force of the rudder and control will be difficult. Add to this the leeway which all yachts make, especially at low speeds, and it becomes obvious that steering a yacht is not quite the same as steering a car. It is perhaps closer to driving a car on a test track with the occasional skid-pan or stretch of gravel!

Another point to consider is how much 'helm' to apply. You only want to turn the rudder by the minimum needed to control the yacht since every time the rudder is significantly off the centre line it is causing drag and slowing you down.

Steering a Compass Course

If required to steer a compass course the average beginner will stare intently at the compass waiting for it to show that the boat is off course. Only then will the mental gymnastics be performed to decide which way to turn the helm before moving the wheel (or tiller).

Because the yacht will not respond instantly, the compass probably continues to show a turn the wrong way. More rudder is then applied and suddenly the yacht is swinging fast, the compass card swings just as violently and you are off course the other way. This leads to a continuous over correction and a very wiggly course.

The way I teach steering a compass course is to start by going back to our analogy of driving a car. If you are going down a motorway at a steady speed, you do not need to stare intently at the speedometer to know that all is well. An occasional glance is all that is necessary, with most of your attention being directed to the road ahead. It is exactly the same for compass course steering.

You need to get roughly on course to start with, noting your initial heading and then

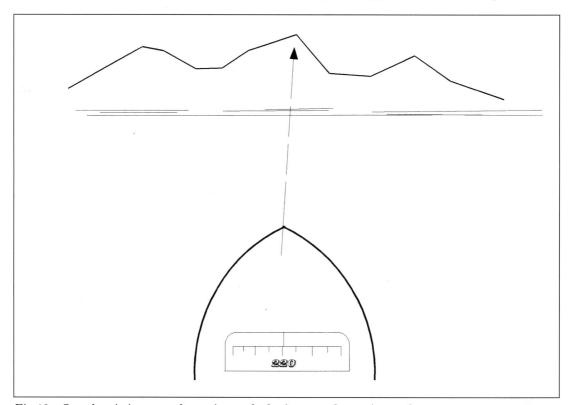

Fig 18   Steer by aiming towards a point on the horizon, not by staring at the compass.

altering course in the right direction while looking ahead at the yacht's bow and the horizon. A couple of glances at the compass should enable you to get on course, with your attention always being directed ahead, out of the yacht.

Once roughly on course, say to within 5 or 10 degrees, you can then gently bring her round, still looking ahead until you are on course and have an aiming point ahead. Keeping on course is then a simple matter of watching the horizon and ensuring that you keep heading towards the same object.

Open Water

Watching the horizon is fine if you can see the land and have something definite to aim for, ideally something a long way off so that its bearing does not change very quickly, but what about when you are in the open sea with no land ahead? In nearly every case the same principle still holds true. However, you need to be prepared to aim for less stable points. You could use a cloud, another yacht more or less directly ahead or, at night, the moon or a star.

All of these objects will obviously change bearing as time passes but this is usually a slow process and it allows you to have a point to aim at for periods of several minutes. Glancing down at the compass will soon tell you when your aiming point has wandered away from the desired compass course. You can then easily adjust back onto course and onto the next aiming point.

In this way your attention is always directed up and forwards and this makes it easier to steer accurately for a number of reasons. Firstly, if a wave or gust of wind pushes the bow one way or the other, it is immediately apparent. There is no delay between the yacht altering course and you as helmsperson being aware of this change. Also, as you apply rudder to correct the swing of the yacht, you can immediately and easily see whether you have

applied enough correction and when to straighten the helm again, without over-shooting your course.

If there are regular waves knocking you off course, it does not take long to get the 'feel' for what each wave does to the yacht. Here there is little point in trying to correct for every tiny movement of the boat, what you are trying to achieve is an average course, not a rock-steady heading.

Very often, the waves will first push the bow one way and then, as the wave passes, push it back the other way again. This allows you to keep a virtually straight helm, letting the yacht wander a little either side of the course but actually averaging a better line than would be possible if you were constantly correcting the small movements.

Similarly, if there is some weather helm and the yacht is always trying to head up into the wind, it should not take long to get the feel of how much helm you need on to counteract this tendency. As a gust hits and the yacht heels over more, it is likely that she will develop more weather helm, while the converse is true in a lull. Looking ahead and watching the swing of the bow across the horizon enables you to counter these variations of force almost instinctively.

At Night

At night it is obviously a little harder to steer than during the day. You must be able to see the compass without straining your eyes all the time otherwise steering will be stressful rather than a pleasure. If it is a very dark night, particularly if it is raining, then it may also be impossible to see the horizon and this obviously makes life still harder.

Even in these none too ideal circumstances, it is still not sensible to attempt to steer by staring at the swinging compass card. Here, you will need to bring into play any factors which might help you – perhaps the angle of the wind to the yacht or how the breeze feels

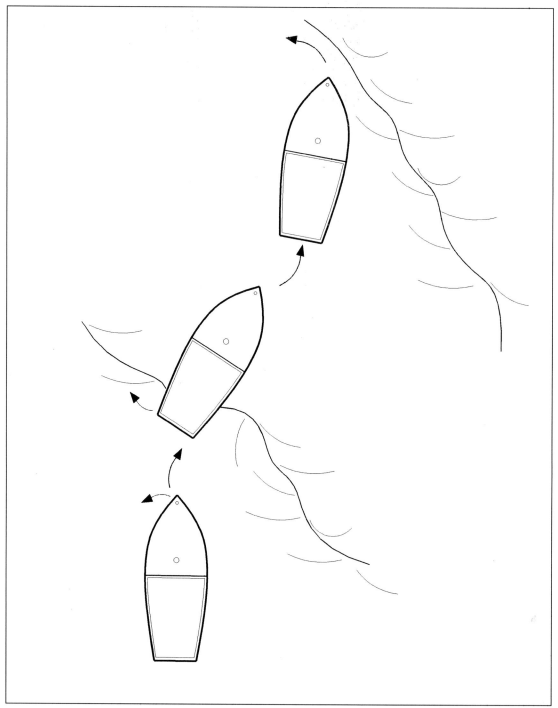

Fig 19   Waves push you a bit either side of course.

on your cheek or ear. Often, the waves will be coming in a regular pattern and at a fairly constant angle to the boat. You can then simply keep the bow pointing at the same angle to the waves as your guide. Once again it is safe to allow every wave to push you a little bit each way without feeling the need for correction.

The only really hard time to steer a compass course is in fog at night, particularly on a calm night where there are few if any waves to give you help. In this situation the tell-tales stick to the headsail in the damp; there is no horizon to look at; little or no wind to feel or, if you are motoring, the wind is always coming from straight ahead no matter which way you turn. Here the only real options are either to go bog-eyed watching the compass or to turn on the autopilot! If forced to hand steer in these circumstances, it will be very important to change the helm on a regular basis since steering will demand so much concentration.

Being a spectacle wearer, I find fog especially difficult because condensation on the lenses makes it hard to see. The matter can be improved slightly by the use of anti-fogging lens cleaners but the only real solution is to

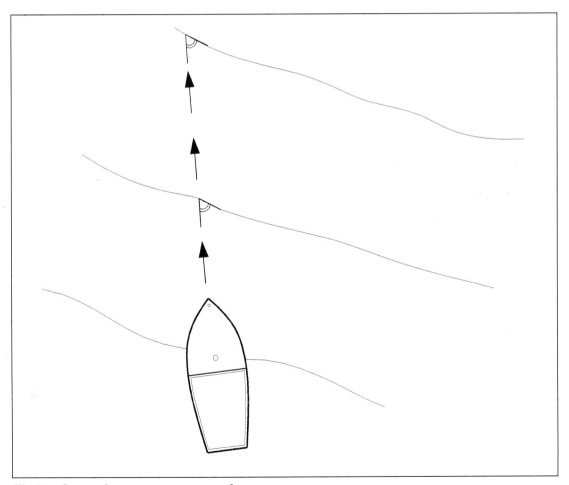

Fig 20   Steer to keep waves at same angle.

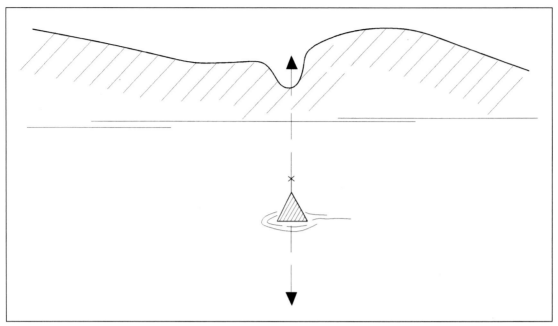

Fig 21   Lining up a pair of transit marks.

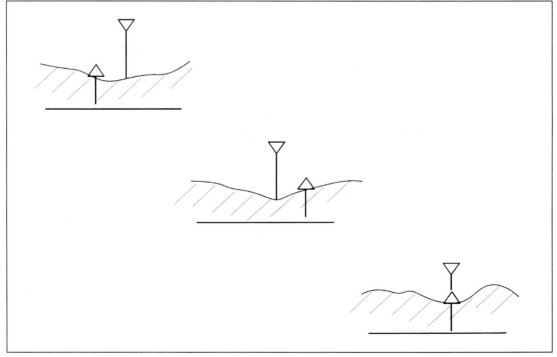

Fig 22   Steering to keep transit lined up.

have some disposable contact lenses ready in case of foggy conditions. Alternatively a plentiful supply of dry tissues will enable you to keep your glasses almost continually dried off.

Steering along a Transit

Transits are very useful when sailing in coastal waters. There are many times when it is necessary to stay on or very close to a particular line as you approach a harbour in order to stay out of danger. In a lot of these cases there will be a leading line or at least two objects which can be lined up to keep you in the channel.

Another time it is useful to sail along a transit line is in racing, when approaching a turning mark in a cross tide. Once again, looking at what the buoy lines up with and keeping the buoy and the other object in line takes you straight to the near point.

In order to keep on the transit, consider which way the nearest point moves relative to the far point. If the near point seems to be moving to the left of the far point, you need to steer a bit to the left to get them lined up again. On the other hand, if the near object is moving to the right of the far one, you need to steer to the right to line them up. In other words, you always steer 'towards the near object' to get the transit lined up again.

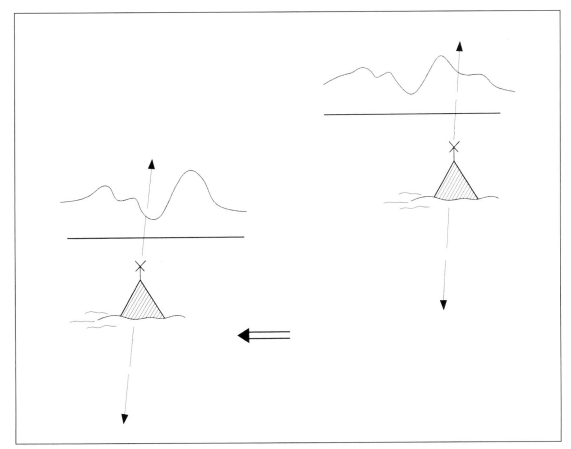

Fig 23   Approaching a mark using a transit.

This assumes that it is the transit itself which is important. In the case of approaching a racing buoy, for example, when you want to track along a straight line to get to the buoy and are using a transit to help, the situation is similar but just a little different.

Here, what is needed is to keep the buoy and the background stationary relative to each other rather than trying to keep the buoy lined up with a particular object in the background. Thus, if you initially find that the buoy is lined up with, say, a building and a few minutes later that building is to the left or right of the buoy, there is no point in trying to steer to get them lined up again. What you should do is find another object to act as a transit and steer to keep them stationary relative to each other.

Upwind Helming

Flat Water

In flat water the important thing to concentrate on while steering is the combination of wind angle and boat speed. Use the luff telltales on the genoa as your steering guide but remember to talk to the genoa trimmer about what you are trying to achieve.

If the boat feels slow or is actually slow then get the trimmer to ease sheets slightly. Similarly, if a patch of rougher water needs to be negotiated, more speed is needed and again the trimmer will need to be asked to ease. Generally, if the water is smooth and the wind fairly steady, it should be possible to get into the groove quite easily.

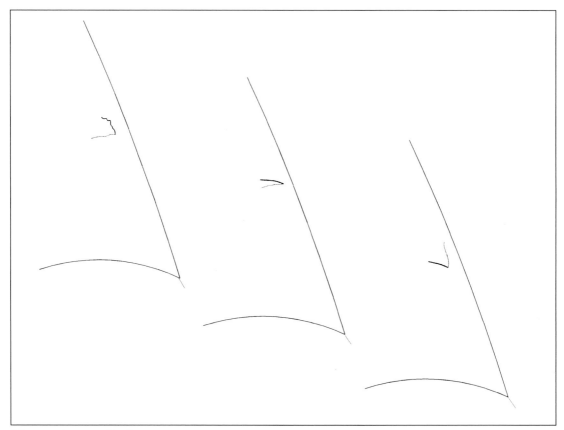

Fig 24   Genoa tell-tales.

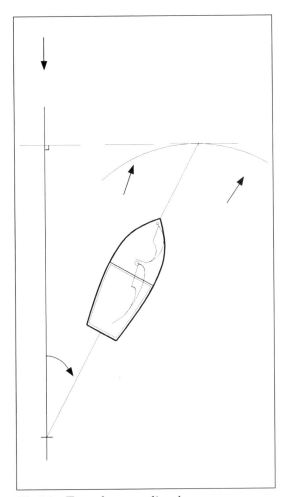

Fig 25   Target boat speed/angle

Target Speeds

If your yacht's performance is well known then using target speeds can be useful. In fact, even if the yacht is relatively unknown to you it is worth keeping a check on the boat speed that seems to be right and then keeping within small limits of that speed – so long as the wind stays constant in strength. If you are using targets, remember that they are the optimum speed and not a speed to be exceeded. If you are sailing faster than your target it probably means that your wind angle is too large and

the resulting VMG (velocity made good) will be less than optimum.

Never steer to maximize your VMG! If you try to do this you will find yourself chasing the VMG up and down like a yo-yo because the inertia inherent in any yacht will delay her response to your steering. Instead, get the trimmers to play with the trim to maximize VMG over a period of, say thirty seconds, then settle on that angle and speed as your target for that wind strength.

Upwind in Waves

Steering upwind in waves calls for a very different approach to that used in flat water. In waves it is always going to be hard to get into a 'target-speed groove' and it is vital that you get a feel for the wave pattern. This means that you must position yourself somewhere that you can easily see the next couple of waves approaching while still being able to see the tell-tales and luff of the headsail. Especially at night it is worth getting another crew member to watch the waves and call any particularly big or nasty shaped ones.

The technique used most often is to attempt to steer the boat so that it points higher up the face of each wave and bears away down the back. This works well because the apparent wind angle moves aft as the bow pitches up and then forward again as the bow goes down. Thus altering the angle to the waves helps to keep the sails giving maximum power at all times.

Although this sounds easy, in practice it is a technique which takes some getting used to. The problem being that you must anticipate what is going to be required a second or two before it is needed and apply the appropriate helm movements before the boat needs to turn.

If you merely wait until the bottom of the trough before starting to point up, it will inevitably be at the top of the crest before the boat will have responded, and vice versa. You

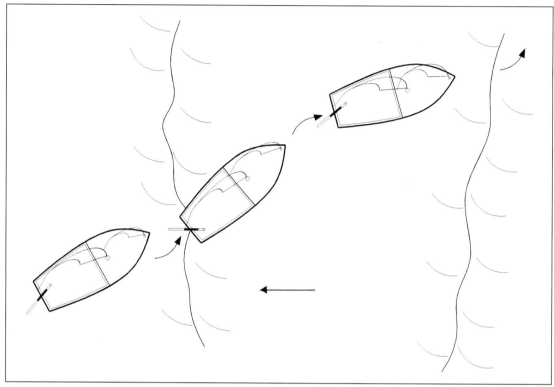

Fig 26   Steering upwind in waves.

will end up being totally out of phase and slower than if you had just kept the helm straight, with the front half of the boat coming out of the water on every wave crest and crashing into the trough.

Target speeds can still be used even in rough water but you need to have a greater tolerance in your idea of the targets. One definite no-no is to attempt to point too high. This will always end up with you being slowed appreciably by the waves. Make sure that the trimmers are setting the sails for a couple of degrees off your flat water angles.

Upwind in Gusty Conditions
In really gusty conditions yet another technique is needed. Here, you will probably have the right sail combination for the average lull and will be overpowered in the gusts and

possibly lacking in power in the worst of the lulls.

You will need to feather the yacht through the gusts rather than trying to keep a straight course which would result in you heeling too much and going sideways. Get the genoa trimmer to sheet in really hard during the gusts, at the same time the mainsheet trimmer will need to drop the traveller down the track. As you feel the yacht coming upright in a lull, bear away slightly, the genoa should be eased at the same time, the traveller brought up and if possible, the backstay also eased a little.

Steering on a Reach
The general principle of steering on a reach is to keep the yacht going as fast as possible while at the same time keeping more or less on the required course. Unless conditions are

very easy and consistent, do not try to keep on an exact compass course but play the waves and gusts/lulls to get the best speeds and a good average course.

Depending on the angle of waves to your course, it may or may not be possible to make use of them for surfing. Experiment a little, trying a few degrees both high and low of the required course to see if it is possible to gain but ensure that the navigator knows what you are doing. There is little point going half a knot faster but thirty degrees off course.

Getting a Tow

In handicap racing it is quite usual for some boats to get to the weather mark ahead of others who will be faster on the reach. In this situation it may be worthwhile attempting to get a tow in the stern wave of the faster boat as she comes past so long as the faster yacht is going to sail approximately the course which you wanted.

To obtain a tow you will need to:

1. get as close to the stern of the larger boat as possible, ideally in her primary stern wave

2. avoid sitting on her wind once you are on the tow

3. make her go to leeward if possible as she overtakes, without slowing her too much unless she is considerably faster than you. This might mean deliberately steering high to allow her to pass several boat lengths to leeward and then bearing away once she is through your dirty air

4. work really hard to keep in her stern wave – not getting overpowered and broaching as her wave picks you up and steering the yacht as if it was a large surf board once you are in her wave

In order to achieve all this it is vital that both the trimmers and tactician understand exactly what you are doing. Once you get on her wave it is too late to start explanations!

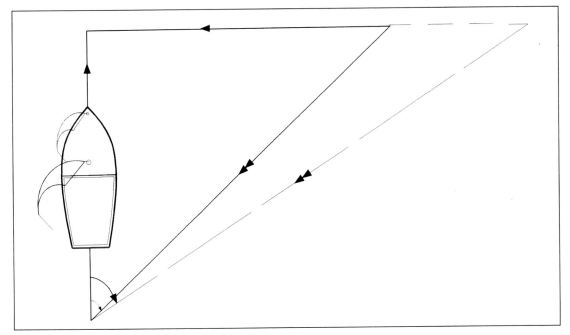

Fig 27   Apparent wind angle changes in a gust.

Reaching in Gusty Conditions

In gusty conditions you must anticipate the gusts before they hit you otherwise you will just heel in each gust, will not accelerate and may even broach. Again, a crew member calling the wind is invaluable.

As a gust approaches, you will need to bear away slightly (with the trimmers easing the sails to suit) and then, as the yacht accelerates in the gust you can gently, ever so gently, come back up to course. The reverse is true in lulls. Here, you will need to luff slightly in order to keep good speed during the lull.

Even if you steer straight during the gusts, the trimmers will need to ease the sheets as the gust hits because the apparent wind will move aft.

Downwind Helming

VMG and Targets Again

Steering on a run we are back to using VMG (for the trimmers) and target speeds and angles for the helm.

In light airs the most important person is the spinnaker trimmer. He (or she) is the one who can feel whether you have enough pressure in the sail to be able to sail squarer to the wind, or if the pressure has dropped making it necessary to luff up for speed. This means that it is crucial to have a good working relationship between the trimmer and the helm who must work together as a team at all times.

Generally you will be trying to sail as low as possible while keeping reasonable speed. As with upwind this will always be a compromise and will change with both wind speed and wave conditions. If you know the performance characteristics of the yacht, sailing to target speeds and angles is nearly always the quickest way downwind.

If your boat speed is above the target speed (from an IMS certificate or previous experience) then you are sailing too high an angle to the wind and should bear away. Similarly, if your boat speed drops below your target speed then you are sailing too low and should luff slightly, at least until the speed starts to rise again.

Get used to using the crew weight to keep the balance feeling right. Heeling to windward can often be faster in lightish airs since it gets the centre of effort of the sails over the keel and reduces the need for rudder to keep the boat going straight. If you are having control problems in stronger winds, keep the boat heeled slightly to leeward as this will help to prevent a leeward broach.

In medium wind strengths, you should be able to sail fairly square while maintaining your target speeds and should have no control

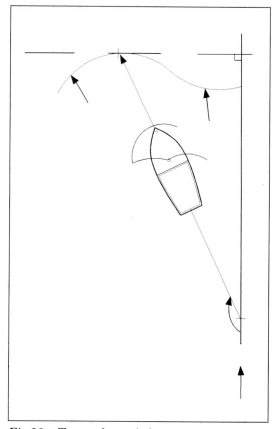

Fig 28   Targets downwind.

problems. However, as the wind increases or becomes more gusty, the loads on the yacht become greater and it therefore takes more work to keep the yacht on track and under control. So long as no one falls off, broaching up to windward is rarely anything more than a noisy, flapping few moments. While it is both slow and does not do the sails much good, nothing is likely to get broken in such a windward broach.

The loss of control which I always hate and which can really cause damage and mayhem is the leeward broach. This should be avoided if at all possible, even at the expense of a little boat speed.

If you are on a square run in strong winds, have a spinnaker up and feel that you are on the verge of losing control, you can stabilise the situation in several ways. Steering slightly high of your course, onto a broad reach, should stop any tendency of the boat to bear away and possibly gybe. Similarly, taking the spinnaker sheet forward and lowering the spinnaker pole should both help to prevent the head of the spinnaker from gyrating and setting up a nasty roll.

Another common cause of leeward broaches is having the kicking strap too loose, allowing the head of the mainsail to twist off too much in each gust. If the mainsheet is right out (as it should be), this means that the top of the mainsail will be heeling the yacht to leeward in the lulls but then to windward as each gust hits. This can change the feel on the helm from weather helm in the lulls to lee helm in the gusts and in itself can cause an accidental gybe.

Surfing
A good helm can make a huge difference to the average boat speed in marginal surfing conditions. As the yacht surfs down a wave, her speed can easily increase by 50 per cent or even more. It is therefore crucial to maintain each surf for as long as possible. As a wave picks up the stern, you should bear away (probably quite sharply) to aim virtually straight down the face of the wave, this will get the yacht pointing downhill and will help to initiate the surf. Once surfing, the next stage is to attempt to stay on the wave for as long as possible. As with a surfer on a Malibu board, this can often be achieved by turning somewhat along the wave to elongate the time before you hit the trough.

As you bear away, the trimmers will need to ease the sheets, then as the yacht accelerates down the wave and the apparent wind moves forward, the sheets will need to be trimmed in again. As at most other times when sailing, the helm and trimmers must work as a team for surfing to be a success.

As part of what you are doing when you surf is to leave the stern wave of the yacht behind, this is one time when you do not want a laminar flow of water over the hull, rudder and keel since this laminar flow will, in effect, be keeping the wave with you. Bearing away sharply might break this flow but it can also sometimes help to jerk the helm several times in order to break the flow away. Obviously, if you do not manage to surf on that particular wave then jerking the helm around is just going to have a slowing effect due to the increased drag as the rudder goes off the centre line.

OFFSHORE MANOEUVRES

Tacking

Tacking is one of the manoeuvres which is carried out so often that most crews just do it without thinking. However, simply because it does happen so often, small improvements in technique can make quite big gains to your overall upwind performance. Obviously, the essence of tacking is to turn the yacht so that she goes through the eye of the wind and

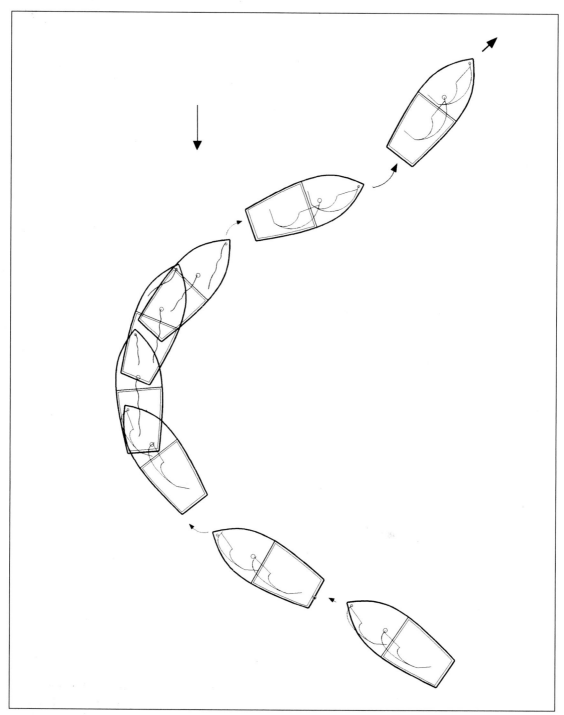

Fig 29   Smooth water tack.

comes out with the sails on the other side. During this time the helmsman can turn fast or slow.

In general terms, it is best to start to turn into the wind quite rapidly, only slowing the turn down once through the eye of the wind although it is worth practising with your own yacht in a variety of conditions to see which loses least speed.

Tacking in smooth water can be carried out fairly rapidly. Certainly the turn towards the wind can be quite fast, unless the wind speed is very low. After a tack it should be possible to bear away accurately to an angle just a degree or so broader than normal, allow the speed to pick up to within a tenth of a knot of target and then harden up to the best angle. Try hard not to overshoot too far as this loses a lot of windward ground for no purpose. If using a big genoa near the top of its range, slow the second half of the tack down to give the winch grinders time to get the sail in.

Tacking in waves should not be a problem. If possible wait for a flat patch before starting to tack and make sure that you have good speed before commencing the turn. If there are no flat bits of water around, try to turn so that the bow is not stopped halfway through by a wave crest. Once through the tack it will be vital to sail slightly low for a short while to allow the yacht to pick up speed again as quickly as possible. since sailing slowly upwind into waves is always very inefficient. Once up to target speed, you can bring the boat back round to her normal angle to the wind, with the trimmers grinding in the last few centimetres of sheet.

Gybing

In my view the person on the helm is by far the most important crew member while gybing. The bowman is often blamed for being too slow when a gybe goes wrong, but a good helm should be able to steer during the gybe

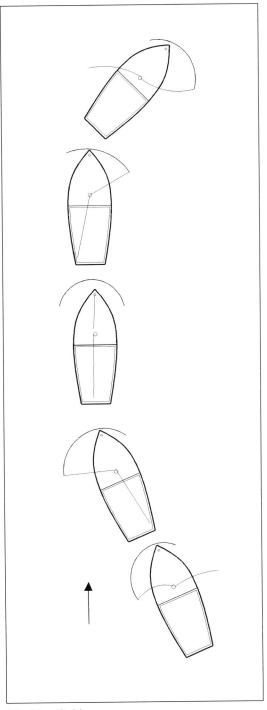

Fig 30   Gybing sequence.

however long it takes for the bowman and other crew to sort out the bits of string.

In anything other than very light air gybes, where the yacht must turn from reach to reach in one continuous and uninterrupted movement, the principles of steering through a gybe are as follows :

1. say 'stand by to gybe' – crew get ready

2. say 'bearing away' – mainsheet come in as the boat bears away. Just before square running call 'trip'

3. crew trip the pole away, trimmer keeps the spinnaker under control and the helm steers to keep the sail filled and to stop it lurching out of control. Do not complete the gybe at this stage

4. when the new guy is in the pole and the pole is squared back, complete the turn smoothly and gybe the mainsail.

Heaving-To

There are times when out in the open sea when all you want to do is stop, perhaps for a few minutes, or even for a couple of hours and this is where heaving-to comes in. The principle behind heaving-to is to balance the forces on the yacht so that she looks after herself with no one worrying about steering or trimming. A by-product is that most yachts heave-to in a manner which quietens down the motion and the noise and makes life pleasantly gentle.

When hove-to, the headsail will be held aback, pressing against the windward shrouds, the helm will be lashed so that it is trying to turn the yacht into the wind and the mainsheet will normally be pulled in as if for close-hauled, with the traveller on the centre line or to leeward. You will need to experiment with your own yacht to see just how hard the headsail sheet should be held aback and how

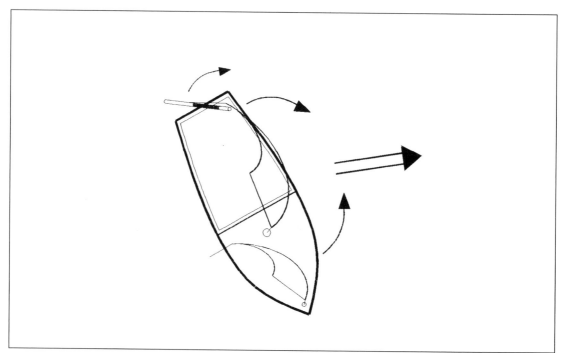

Fig 31 Equilibrium while hove-to.

far over the helm needs to be in order to achieve equilibrium. If the wind changes strength these controls will need adjustment.

The yacht will heel to leeward a bit, but not so much as when sailing close-hauled since there is less effective pressure on the sails and she will 'fore-reach' at anything from half a knot upwards. Fore-reaching means that she will make good a course just forward of a beam reach, moving forward a little and sideways a lot.

The easiest way to get into the hove-to position, is to be sailing close-hauled on the

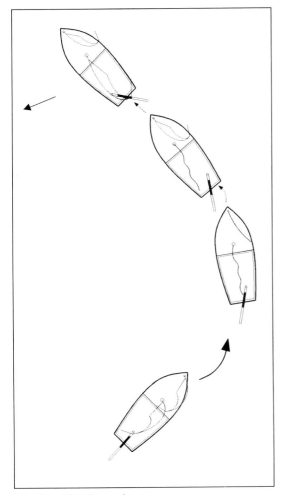

Fig 32   Tacking to heave-to.

tack you do not want to heave-to on. Ease the headsail sheet slightly and then tack, leaving the sheets secure where they were. This will leave the headsail aback. As soon as she is through the wind, straighten the helm otherwise the yacht will continue turning and will eventually gybe.

Once she has settled with the headsail aback on the new tack, gently apply helm to turn her into the wind. You should come to a point where the helm is as far over as possible without there being any danger of the yacht actually tacking. This is your ideal, hove-to position for that wind strength. You should now be able to lash the helm and leave the boat to her own devices while you put in a reef, have a meal, or use the heads.

Because whilst hove-to, you are still subject to the normal 'rules of the road', it makes sense whenever possible to heave-to on the starboard tack. This only leaves you vulnerable to yachts who are also on a starboard tack but who are pointing or sailing higher than you and even with these, it is likely that they will be overtaking you and will therefore have to keep clear.

MAN OVERBOARD

The general principle should be that a man overboard is potentially lethal and should be avoided if at all possible! Even on a nice day, in reasonable conditions and with a strong crew, anyone in the water is at severe risk of drowning or being injured. At the very least, even if a prompt recovery is executed, the person is likely to be in shock – believe me it is pretty frightening both to see the yacht from which you have just involuntarily departed sailing away and also to see her coming back, probably at speed and aiming right for you.

Having said the above, even with the best safety attitude in the world, accidents can still happen and it is relatively common for a crew member to fall overboard. It is therefore important that all crew members know the procedures to be followed to allow for a safe recovery.

The critical parts of man overboard recovery are:

1. not losing sight of the person

2. keeping the person afloat until you get back

3. manoeuvring the yacht to get back as fast as possible

4. being able to stop alongside the person when you return

5. being prepared to ask for assistance if needed

Taking these critical points one at a time, the first obvious requirement is that you maintain contact with the person in the water, preferably visual contact. This means that if someone does fall in, one crew member should do nothing but keep an eye on the person. Pointing with an outstretched arm helps to keep focused, especially if the person keeps going out of sight behind waves.

At night it is obviously even harder to keep an eye on the person unless he has a torch or emergency light with him. If you do lose sight of the person in the water then the sound of a whistle can help in re-establishing contact.

Keeping the person afloat is really about safety on board. If conditions are such that the yacht is bouncing all over the place and a man overboard is a realistic possibility, it is probably worth most crew members wearing a life jacket or buoyancy aid when on deck. In any case there should be a lifebuoy within easy reach of the helmsman and ready for instant deployment.

If you have a man overboard do not hesitate to throw this lifebuoy into the water – as close to the person as possible. My own experiences have shown me that seeing the person holding

onto a lifebuoy and obviously being safe for a few minutes takes most of the stress out of the situation.

Manoeuvring the yacht back to the person as fast as possible does not necessarily mean spinning her round instantly. This is quite likely to disorientate the crew, may cause actual damage or chaos on board and is very unlikely to get you back to the person in the water in a position from which you could pick him up. This is very much a case for more speed less haste!

However you turn the yacht, it should be in a planned and organized way so that you not only avoid damage (to yacht or to other crew members) but also so that once you have done the manoeuvre, you are in a position to get back to the person as fast as possible.

Being able to stop the vessel when you get alongside the person in the water is essential. If the yacht is travelling at any speed over about half a knot, it will be virtually impossible for the waterlogged person to hold on, either to a hand or rope. This means that the sails must either be down or flapping as you return.

It is important to realise that this is a potentially life-threatening accident. It may be that all goes well and you manage to return to the person in the water after a few minutes and have no difficulty getting him back on board. However, it does not take much for the situation to turn very ugly indeed and if anything goes wrong it may, by that time, be too late to call for outside assistance.

If there are other yachts or motor vessels close to hand or if you are within reasonable distance of a lifeboat station or helicopter rescue base, then it may be worthwhile sending off a Mayday call on the radio as soon as the person has fallen in. If all goes well and he is recovered, this call can always be cancelled.

As far as the actual manoeuvre used is concerned, it does not really matter how you get back to the person in the water so long as

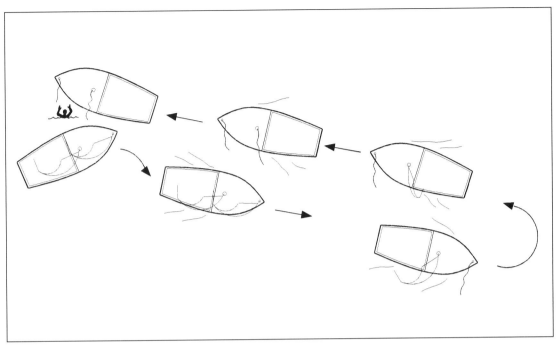

Fig 33 Reach-tack-reach MOB recovery.

it is in a controlled, relatively quick and total-ly reliable way. Each yacht and virtually every point of sailing will give its own 'best' method. However, unless you are extremely experi-enced and can operate well even under severe pressure, I would suggest that you adopt a 'standard' man overboard recovery method which will suffice for any and every situation. The following paragraphs look at the two most common manoeuvres in use.

Reach-Tack-Reach Method

The essence of the reach-tack-reach manoeuvre is that it enables the crew to keep the yacht under total control at all times, it does not require any violent changes in course which may disorientate the remaining crew and it can be done without the use of the engine. The chief disadvantage of the method is that, especially on a large, fast yacht, it is

likely that you will have travelled for a fair distance before turning round to return to the person in the water.

As can be seen from the diagrams, the basic plan will be to turn the yacht onto a beam reach to the apparent wind as quickly as possible – that is to bear away to a beam reach if sailing close-hauled or to come up to a beam reach if previously broad reaching or running.

Once on a reach, the yacht is prepared for a tack as quickly as is reasonably possible. If you had a spinnaker up then this must be dropped first and if there was a preventer on the main boom this will need to be removed or let go before tacking.

The yacht is then tacked through 180 degrees when she should be pointing directly at the person in the water. If the initial reach was actually a beam reach to the apparent wind, the new course will be a close reach with the wind a little forward of the beam. The

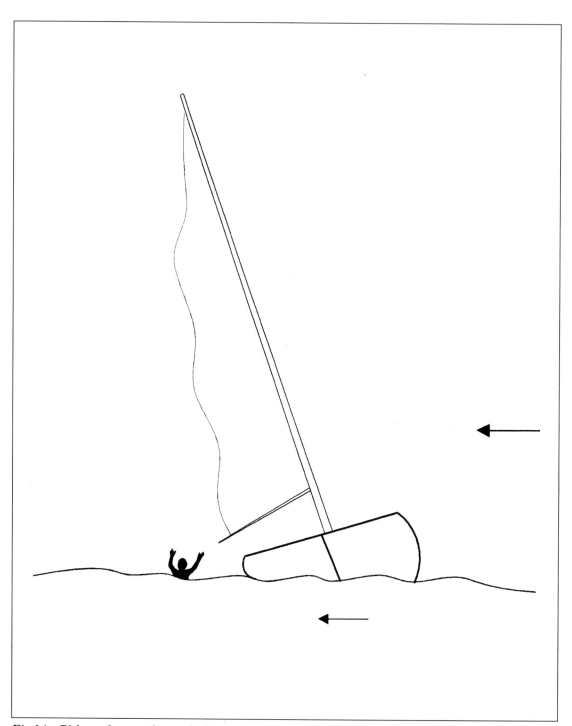

Fig 34   Pick up the casualty on the leeward side.

headsail (if set) should now be let fly and the mainsail should also be let right out.

Next comes the only potentially tricky part of the whole manoeuvre. If at this stage, while pointing back at the victim, the mainsail does not flap when let out, the yacht is too far upwind. In this case a rapid and positive bear away for a boat length or two, followed by pointing her once again at the victim should correct the situation.

On the other hand, if the yacht is almost close-hauled when pointing back at the victim, there is the real possibility that you will not be able to get back to him without tacking unless steps are taken early enough to rectify the situation. Sail as high to the wind as you can for a few boat lengths to gain windward gauge and then point at the victim once more.

As can be seen, the idea is to end up, several boat lengths away from the victim, so that the yacht can sail on a close reach towards the victim, neither so far to windward that you cannot slow down nor so far downwind that you struggle to 'lay' the victim.

Once you are happy with the position of the yacht, leave the headsail flapping (or possibly furl it or even drop it if you have enough crew) and approach the victim slowly, controlling the speed of the yacht with just the mainsheet. You should aim to put the victim to leeward of the yacht and no more than three metres away. This is to make it easier for the victim to get back on board and to enable you to finish several metres away in safety, drifting slowly down to him and being able to throw lines or a lifebuoy to him downwind.

As you get to the person in the water, all way should be taken off the yacht by letting go of the mainsheet and possibly turning a little more into the wind.

While this manoeuvre does not rely at all on the use of an engine, it can be very reassuring to have one available if this is both possible and easy. If you do use the engine, either to gain a bit of windward gauge or to slow down,

be very careful that there are no warps or sheets in the water which might get caught in the propeller. Obviously, ensure that the engine is firmly in neutral or turned off when close to the victim or else severe injury could result.

When you have the person alongside, the next problem will be to get him (or her) back on board. Even a fairly fit person will normally have difficulty in climbing aboard unaided if they have been in cold water for more than one or two minutes.

If the freeboard is reasonably low and the person in the water is fit, then it should not be too hard to manhandle him in over the side. One arm and one leg followed by a roll onto the sidedeck often suffices. However, there will be times, when the person is heavy and/or unfit or the freeboard is particularly high, when mechanical means will be needed to get the person back on board.

If you have an inflated dinghy then this makes an easy stepping platform. If the weather is not too rough and the yacht has a bathing platform at the stern then this can be used, but beware in rough weather for the sharp edges of the transom will be bouncing up and down a fair bit and can be quite dangerous.

If all else fails, a halyard can be used, either direct onto a winch or possibly with a four or six to one handy billy at the end. If the person is conscious and not too cold, then a bowline tied under their arms is all that is needed unless they are wearing a safety harness when this can be used.

A point to be aware of in cases of suspected hypothermia, is that hauling a person on-board like this could easily end up killing them as the combination of pressure on their chest and their blood rushing from their body core down into their legs causes a drop in blood pressure. In this case a horizontal lift is needed, possibly with one rope under their arms and another behind their knees.

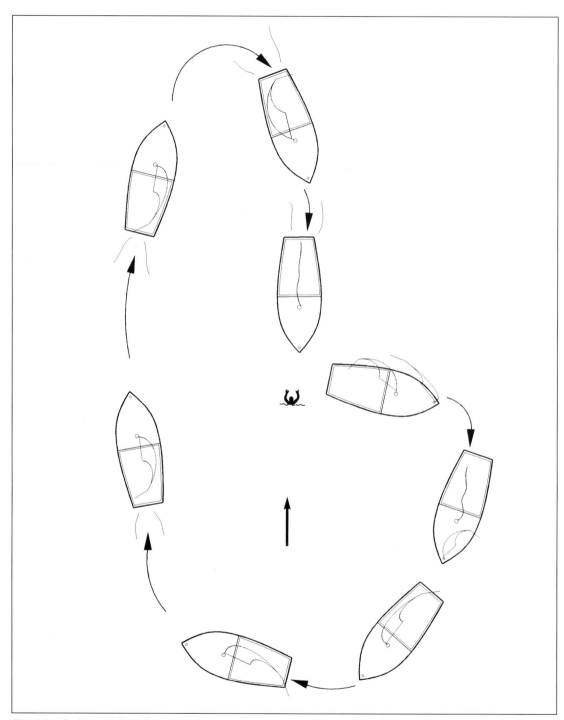

Fig 35 Quick stop MOB recovery.

Quick Stop Method

The 'quick stop' method of man overboard recovery uses quite different principles to the reach-tack-reach method. Its main feature is that the yacht never goes very far away from the victim.

As soon as possible after the person has fallen overboard, the yacht is immediately tacked, regardless of which sails you have up at the time. Once through the wind, the yacht is held effectively hove to, almost head to wind.

Having stopped, the next move is to sort out the foredeck, getting rid of the headsail, spinnaker and anything else necessary as quickly as possible.

The mainsail is then pinned amidships and the engine started. The yacht is driven, with the main pinned in, to a position dead downwind of the victim and is then motored straight towards the victim. Once alongside the remainder of the recovery is exactly the same as for the reach-tack-reach.

While this quick stop method is advocated by a great many experienced skippers and instructors, I have never liked it for three reasons. Firstly, it relies pretty heavily on the engine starting. Secondly, it necessitates crew getting rid of headsails as a must, rather than as a nicety and this can cause real problems if short-handed or if a halyard snags. Lastly, the initial tack can be a very extreme manoeuvre, especially if you were running when the person fell in the water. It can lead to damage or to disorientation and possibly to losing sight of the victim, especially at night.

3

MOORING AND BERTHING UNDER POWER

SWINGING MOORINGS

No Tide

This is one of the simplest of all mooring situations. The approach needs to be made so that, in the event of overshooting the buoy, the yacht can be safely manoeuvred around again. If there is really no tide then the approach should be more or less into the wind.

If there has been a headsail left on the fore-deck then it is easiest for the crew if the approach is made with the buoy on the opposite side. On most yachts the bow itself is quite hard to work from, with the constrictions of the forestay and stemhead fitting. It is therefore generally best to try to stop the yacht with the buoy resting alongside the side of the boat, about two to three metres along from the very bow.

In case the yacht still has way on when the buoy is alongside, it is safest to have the bow turned slightly away from the wind with the buoy on the windward side of the bow. In this way if the crew fail to get the buoy, the yacht will blow away from the buoy with no danger of the buoy or its cable going under the boat and wrapping around the keel or rudder.

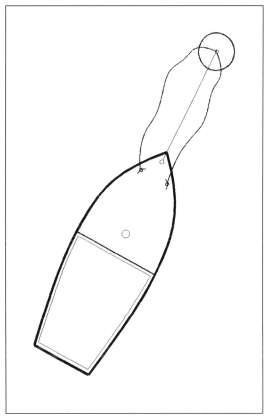

Fig 36   Rig a slack slip rope as back up and for letting go.

Make sure that the crew is ready with either a boat-hook or warp. If possible choose a buoy which has a pick-up strop as this makes life very easy. If this is not possible, it is often simplest to use a bight of rope to lasso the buoy, making fast properly after the boat has stopped. The hardest way for the crew on most modern, high sided yachts, is for them to try to get hold of the top of the buoy and thread a warp through it while the yacht is still unsecured.

One piece of equipment which can make life simpler is a patent hook on the end of the boathook which slides off once it is fixed to the buoy, leaving a warp already attached by the hook.

As the buoy is approached, the helmsman will almost certainly lose sight of it in the last few metres. It is therefore important that the crew are briefed to give either voice or hand signals to indicate the position of, and distance from the buoy.

In light conditions it is no problem to approach the buoy at low speed, allowing the natural way of the yacht to fall off and needing hardly any reverse gear to stop. If the wind is stronger then more speed will be required in order to maintain steerage-way and prevent the bow from falling off downwind. In really strong conditions it may be necessary to approach directly into the wind to prevent this happening, but beware of running over the buoy.

Once an initial line has been attached to the buoy, the yacht can be moored more securely. Unless there is a strong line attached to the buoy, preferably with a swivel between line and buoy, you will have to use your own lines.

I like to take two separate ropes to the buoy, one of these would normally lead over the bow roller and be attached with a round turn and bowline. The second safety line can be rigged as a loose slip-rope, going from the port side, through the fairlead, through the ring of the buoy and back up through the starboard fairlead. This must be kept looser than the main mooring rope otherwise it is likely to chafe. The advantage of this arrangement is that, when you wish to leave, the slip-rope can be tightened, the other rope cast off and then the slip-rope can easily be released when required.

If leaving the yacht on a mooring for a long time it is worth rigging an anti-chafe piece of hosepipe around the main mooring line where it goes over the bow roller. Large and heavy yachts may well use the end of their anchor chain as the safety line since this will be immensely secure. It is normally best to use rope for the main, tight mooring rope since this will give more and be less likely to snatch under load.

Wind With Tide

This is in some ways even easier than mooring with no tide. The basic approach is more or less the same and all that has been said about actually tying the yacht up still applies. The chief difference is that, since you will be approaching into both wind and tide, there will be more steerage-way at low speeds thus making it easy to stop at the buoy.

Here, as in most mooring situations, the approach should be arranged so that you are virtually heading into the tide and being blown off slightly by the wind. Unless the wind and tide are exactly in line, this may limit your approach to one tack only. In other respects, this is the same situation as if there was no tide.

Wind Against Tide

In this situation, the basic difference is that the yacht will lie, either head-to-tide or somewhere near this position once the mooring has been secured. However, the wind will make it harder to slow down and stop as you approach the buoy.

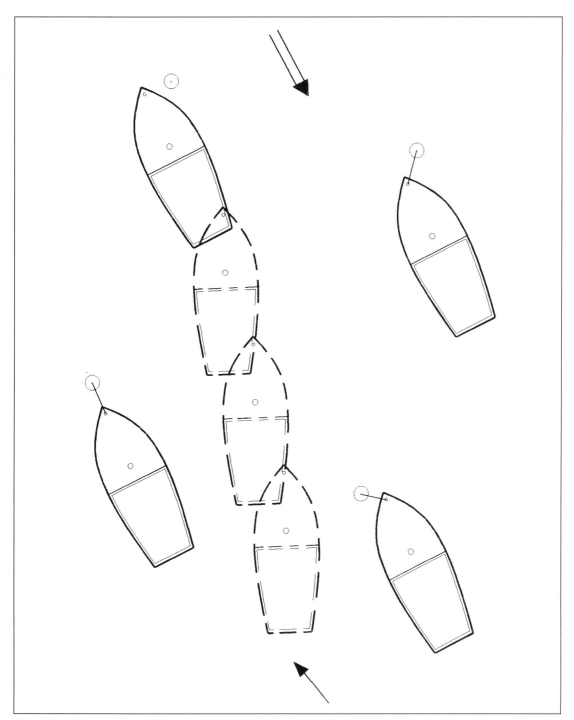

Fig 37   Use other moored boats to judge your approach angle.

The ideal is to approach the mooring point-ing in the direction that you will end up facing once secured. In most cases, except where the tide is weak and the wind strong, this will mean facing into the tide.

Ideally, look at other yachts moored close by to help you in your judgement as to how you will end up lying. When doing this make sure that you are comparing other yachts similar to your own since heavy, deep-draught, low-freeboard yachts will lie almost directly into the tide while lighter, high-freeboard or shallow-draught yachts will be affected more by the wind.

Often, if the wind and tide are in direct opposition, the yacht will end up pointing into the tide but overriding the buoy as she is pushed forward by the wind. If you think this is likely then it will tell you that you will need reverse gear to stop completely and that there is a real danger of being blown onto the buoy if you approach too fast. You will need to make sure that if you do overrun, you are blown away from the buoy.

If you cannot decide exactly how you will end up lying once secured to the buoy, the safest approach will be to head directly into the tide as you come towards the buoy, with the buoy on your windward side. Once again this ensures that if you make a mistake the yacht will not be blown onto or over the buoy.

Wind Across Tide

This is really a variation of the wind against tide situation. However, with the wind blowing across the tide, there will less danger of getting the mooring wrapped around the keel or rud-der, so long as you approach into the tide and with the buoy to windward.

From a yacht handling point of view, it will be necessary to maintain slightly more boat speed than usual in order to keep the yacht from making a lot of leeway. It will probably also be necessary to make your approach

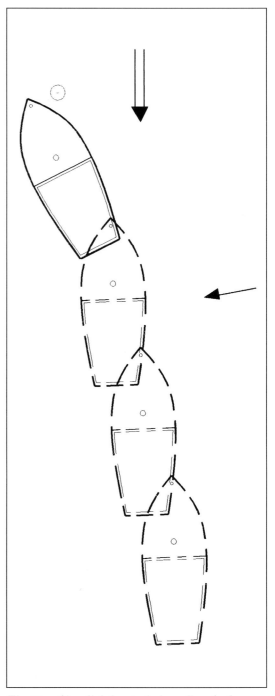

Fig 38 Aim slightly upwind to allow for leeway and jink to leeward at the last moment.

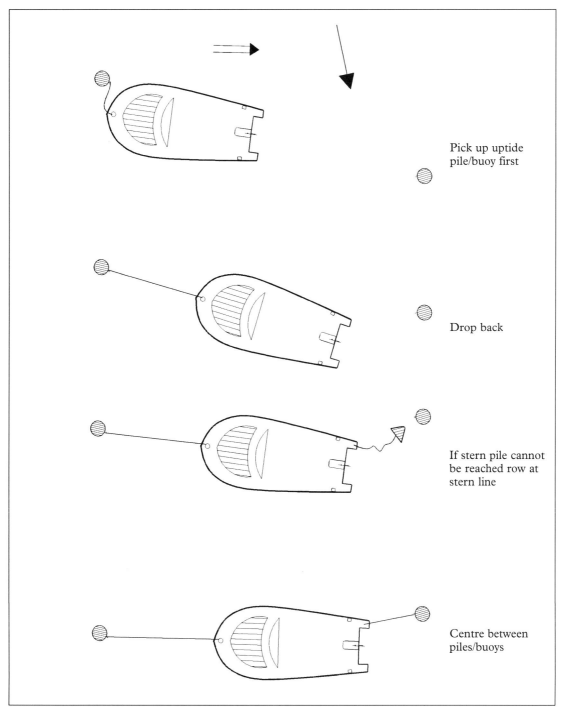

Pick up uptide
pile/buoy first

Drop back

If stern pile cannot
be reached row at
stern line

Centre between
piles/buoys

Fig 39   Fore and aft mooring – wind across tide. A simple method.

aiming slightly into the wind to counteract leeway. You then need to swing the bow around in the last metre or two to get the buoy on the windward side.

The temptation is to approach as above but then to keep aiming slightly into the wind for the pick-up, leaving the buoy to leeward. While this may seem easier, it leaves you in the dangerous situation of being blown onto the buoy and thus potentially getting its ground tackle wrapped around the boat if you overshoot or need to go around again for any reason.

FORE AND AFT MOORINGS

Simplest Method

If picking up either pile moorings or buoys where you will eventually lie with one at the bow and one at the stern then there are several ways of executing the manoeuvre. The simplest although not the most elegant, is to tie up to the upstream pile or buoy first, in exactly the same way as if there was only one mooring point. Once ready you can then row a line to the other pile or buoy and pull the yacht central between them.

Unless wind and tide are almost exactly in line, it is not normally possible to tie to the upstream mooring, and then simply drop back to the other mooring since manoeuvring in reverse with the bow made fast is very difficult at the best of times and often impossible.

If you decide to use this simple method, it is very important to check beforehand that you will lie clear of other yachts or obstructions during the time you are only moored by the bow. For this reason, this is not a safe manoeuvre to try if the wind and tide are working against each other since it is then very hard to ascertain exactly how the yacht will lie. Similarly, if the wind is blowing across the line of the piles, there must obviously be enough

room to leeward so that your yacht does not foul any other boats in another row of piles.

Most pile moorings have a vertical metal riser attached on each side, with a large ring sliding up and down on the riser. The ring is usually, but not always, attached to the top of the riser either with a rope or light chain. This allows you to pull the ring up to within reach even at high tide.

If you plan to stay on the piles for only a short time, then as with making fast to a buoy, a slip-rope is the easiest way to attach the yacht. In this case it is not at all important to tie to the ring, since you will not be there long enough for the tide to come in or go out significantly and rigging a slip through the riser is perfectly sufficient.

If the intention is to moor to the piles for more than a short time and there is any tidal rise or fall anticipated, then you should eventually use the ring since this avoids chafe on the riser. For the same reason, slip-ropes should not be used except for short stays and the bow and stern should be made fast in the same way as to a buoy, with a round turn and a bowline. If you make the loop of the bowline quite long, say one to two metres, then you will not need to pull the yacht right up to the pile when you come to leave.

If I am leaving a yacht on piles unattended, or if it is very windy, then I will always use two warps at the bow and a further two at the stern if at all possible. The second warps are there as safety lines, just in case the primary warp chafes through or snaps. For permanent pile moorings it is worth having warps with hard eyes spliced into the outer end which can be shackled to the ring since this virtually eliminates chafe.

Running Moor

Wind With Tide

The running moor is a slightly more complicated but much more elegant way of making fast to fore and aft pile or buoy moorings. The basic principle of the running moor is to approach from downtide, make the stern fast to the downtide pile as you motor slowly past it, and then to motor up to the upstream pile while paying out slack on the stern line. Once both moorings have been attached it is a simple matter to drop back centrally between the piles.

In practice it is not too difficult so long as a few simple rules are followed but there is considerable scope for error and confusion. The main requirement for a successful running moor is a long enough warp. When it is attached to your stern it should allow you to motor to the other pile and still return some slack. It is possible to use a slip-rope on the stern pile but in my experience this causes more problems than it solves.

A long warp should be made ready at the stern in preparation for the mooring. This should be made fast to a cleat in such a way that in an emergency it can be released completely. The other end of the warp should be taken through a fairlead and up to a point around amidships ready for tying to the pile. The rest of the warp needs to be coiled or flaked out so that it can be paid out without snagging.

A shortish bow line also needs to be prepared, again with the inboard end made fast to a cleat and the other end taken out through a fairlead. Both of these warps should be on the upwind side. If you have enough crew, a roving fender can be useful, particularly if the piles are made of rusty steel.

The yacht should then be motored slowly up to the downstream pile approaching on the side that allows the wind to blow you away from the pile. The aim should be to almost stop the yacht with the pile a little forward of amidships, keeping just enough way on her to give steerage.

As the pile comes within reach, the stern line can be tied to it, ideally using a round turn and a bowline to the ring, but *in extremis*, any

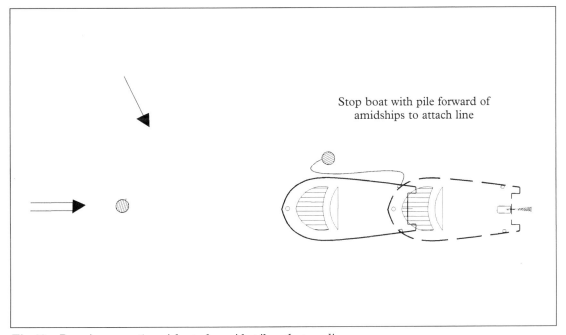

Stop boat with pile forward of amidships to attach line

Fig 40   Running moor 1 – pick up downtide pile wth stern line.

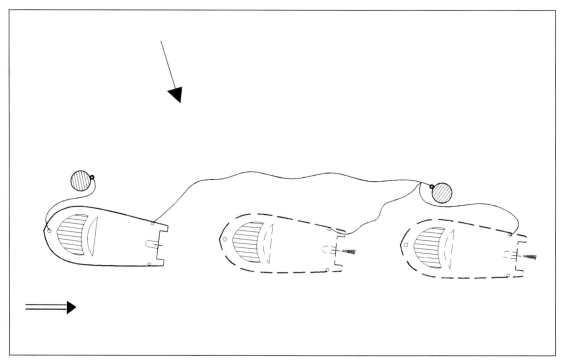

Fig 41   Running moor 2 – motor to uptide pile keeping stern line slack.

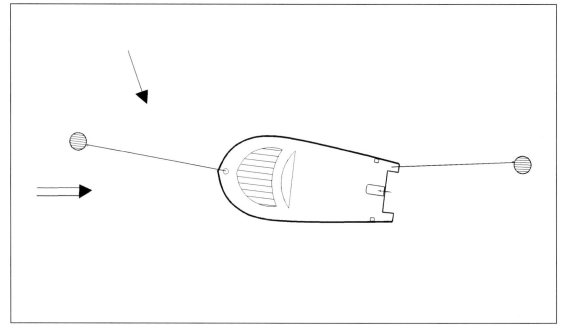

Fig 42   Running moor 3 – centre between piles.

secure knot to either the ring or the riser will suffice. The crew member attaching this line should be told that the yacht may still be moving and be prepared to make fast while walking slowly down the deck if necessary.

A little more power and the yacht is motored up to the second pile, with the stern line being paid out and kept slack as you go forward. If the stern line snags or is held tight then it will 'wag' the stern and prevent you from steering so slackness is vital.

As the second pile is approached, the person at the bow needs to call out distance and ideally, you should stop with the pile about one to two metres down the upwind side of the bow. Once there, the pile can be held onto to keep it from touching the yacht's side and the bow line made fast. I say stop with the pile back from the stem because it is easiest for the crew member working there to do so over the side rather than over the bow.

Once both lines are made fast, the yacht can be centred. If two warps are going to be used at either bow, stern or both, then these can be secured either by pulling the yacht to each pile in turn or by rowing the second ropes out once you are secure.

Similarly, if the intention is to stay for only a short time, it is often easiest to rig a slip rope on the bow as you first make fast and then to drop back immediately to the stern pile and change the warp for a slip-rope at this stage. If you leave this job until just before you intend to depart, the odds are that another yacht will come and moor alongside making the rigging of a slip that much harder!

Wind Against or Across Tide

In essence this is no different to the wind with tide situation. In a wind across tide you must have the piles on the windward side if at all possible and if this is not achievable then you must be prepared to have at least one or two crew available to fend off the piles, especially the stern one.

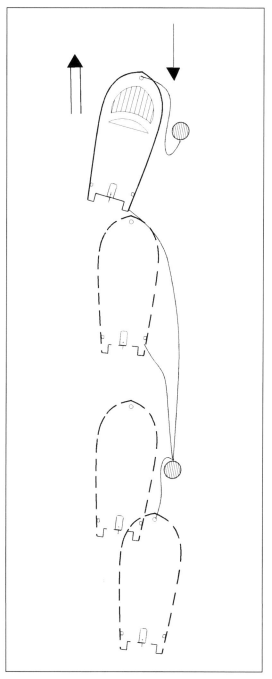

Fig 43 Running moor – strong wind versus weak tide. Pick up downwind pile first but do not stop.

If the wind and tide are in direct opposition then although you would normally still pick up the downstream pile first, there will be times when the tide is weak and the wind strong, when it is best to make your approach into the wind instead of into the tide.

If you are forced into a downtide approach, remember that in order to maintain steerageway you will have to be moving through the water and your speed over the ground will be that much greater – thus the crew member tending the stern line will have to be a bit quicker in tying up the knot.

Pile Moorings

If you are going to tie to pile or other fore and aft moorings and there is already another yacht lying to the selected pair, then the procedure is exactly the same as if the other yacht was moored to a pontoon. First come alongside the yacht and moor with breast ropes and springs. Then, when secure, row lines out to the piles and secure to these as well.

If you do not have access to a dinghy then life is made slightly more complicated. It may be possible to tie temporarily to the other yacht and then, once relatively secure, spring or pull your own yacht to each pile in turn, securing head and stern ropes while there.

In some circumstances it may be easier and safer to execute a running moor on the piles before securing to the other yacht – the state of wind and tide and the position of the other yacht in relationship to the piles will determine which approach is best. However, if you do have access to a dinghy, it will nearly always be safest to moor alongside first.

Leaving Pile Moorings

If moored alongside another yacht while lying to piles the procedure for leaving is exactly the same as for any other alongside berth

Yachts tied to pile moorings.

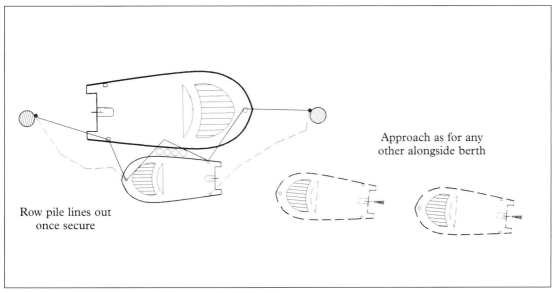

Fig 44 Pile mooring alongside another boat.

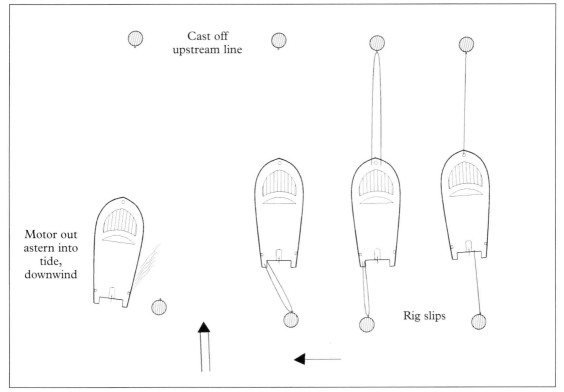

Fig 45 Leaving a for and aft mooring, facing downtide.

situation. The only small difference is that your own lines to the piles will need to be removed before leaving, much as shore lines would need to be removed if lying outside another yacht on a quay.

If on a pair of piles on your own, the things to remember are as follows. First, rig up slip-ropes to both piles so that it is possible to leave without the need to come close to either pile. In nearly every situation it will be better and safer to leave in the direction which is against the tide. This may be forwards or in astern depending on the direction of the current. As a general principle, leaving downtide should be avoided if at all possible because of the danger of hitting any yachts which are moored close to you on the downtide pile before you have got steerage-way.

If your vessel handles really badly astern and you are moored so that the current is facing your stern it may be worth considering swinging (or winding) the yacht around so that you are still attached to the piles but are now facing into the current – swinging ship is covered separately. This will be particularly likely if the wind and current are in opposition. You will probably still need to leave the piles astern but the wind on the bow is likely to blow the bow off and make it harder to steer.

Taking the most common situation, rig the slip-ropes and warm the engine up so that there is no danger of it stalling. Then let go the downtide slip and motor towards the uptide pile. As the other slip goes slack release that as well. In deciding which way to leave, always try to manage it so that the wind is blowing you away from danger – most probably the piles in this case.

MOORING ALONGSIDE

For most people sailing nowadays, coming alongside a marina pontoon is the commonest berthing manoeuvre. With practice it is relatively easy in most situations but as with all things there are some basic principles which help to make it easier.

If possible arrange life so that you approach the berth facing into the tide. This means that stopping is simpler but more importantly that you will be able to maintain steerage way while going very slowly over the ground.

Obviously there will be times when this is not possible, for example when returning to your permanent marina berth downtide. Unless you are confident of your boat handling abilities, it may be better in this situation to berth elsewhere temporarily, moving to your allocated pontoon when conditions are easier.

Think about the prop-walk of your yacht. If she kicks the stern to port when you put her in astern then a port side berth will generally be easier than one which is starboard side. This is because as you put the engine in reverse to stop, the stern will swing to port – towards the pontoon if it is on your port side but away from the berth if it is to starboard.

If there is a strong cross wind then this too will affect which side is easier to berth. It is always much simpler to get alongside if the wind is blowing you onto the berth than if it is blowing off and this can easily nullify any prop-walk.

Line the yacht up from as far away as possible so that you are not going to need to do any unnecessary sharp turns in the last few metres when you should be travelling slowly and will therefore have less control. Try not to put her actually onto the berth, rather aim to have the yacht between 30cm (12in) to 60cm (24in) off when you are alongside – this should be close enough for the crew to step off but far enough away so that there is no danger of scraping the topsides.

If the wind is blowing you away from the berth you can afford to be closer initially. However if there is a strong wind blowing you onto the berth, then you can and should aim to be even further away, the wind will then carry you gently sideways onto the berth.

Ropework

So far as tying up is concerned, the purpose of the various ropes has already been covered in the chapter dealing with general yacht handling manoeuvres. What we need eventually is a bow and stern line plus bow and stern springs, with some of these doubled up if it is really windy.

If berthed at the inboard end of a pontoon with a tee piece going across at right angles to the pontoon in front of the yacht, it is worth having a second bow line going across to the tee, on the opposite side of the yacht from the pontoon. This will help to keep the yacht parallel to the pontoon and allows both bow lines to be kept quite slack.

Initially however, we neither need nor can cope with all four or five of these lines and therefore some thought should be put into which lines are most urgent. If coming alongside really short-handed then it may only be feasible to get one line ashore at first. In this case the best line to use is a short warp from just forward of amidships to an immediately adjacent cleat.

If there are two of you on the yacht, this warp can be taken ashore and made fast by 'the crew' while the helmsman steers the yacht to keep her parallel to the pontoon. A touch of forward propulsion will be needed if the wind and/or tide are against you or a touch of astern if berthing downwind/downtide.

Because the line is made fast to the widest part of the yacht and about at the natural pivot point, it should allow quite good steering even when stationary. This is especially true in forward gear, when you can use the thrust

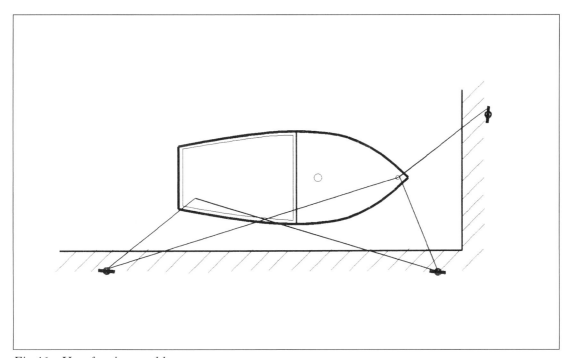

Fig 46   Use of springs and breast ropes.

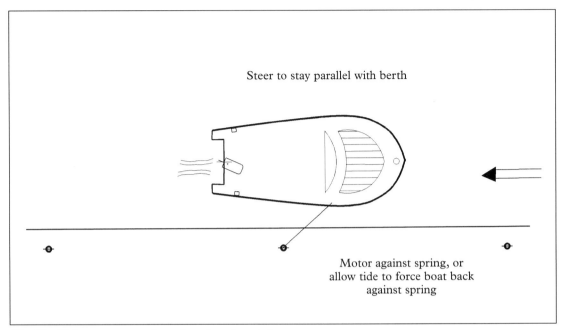

Steer to stay parallel with berth

Motor against spring, or
allow tide to force boat back
against spring

Fig 47   Using a centre spring when short-handed.

from the propeller to work against the pull of
the warp.

Once the centre line is made fast (quite
short and tight if possible), the crew can take
their time to get first head and stern breast
ropes on, then whichever spring is actually
needed to counteract the tide at present, and
finally the other spring and any ancillary warps
you might want. In most situations you will
want to remove the centre warp once made
fast properly since it is deliberately short and
is likely to snub as the yacht bounces up and
down on passing wash from other boats.

If you have more crew available then a
decision needs to be made as to which lines to
get them to take ashore first. A centre line is
still often a good idea, even if you have lots of
crew who can leap ashore each with a line but
it is obviously far less important than when
short-handed.

Generally, a bow line, stern line and
working spring will be the best option if you
can get three lines ashore at once. If only two

are possible then just one from the bow and
another from the stern is probably best, with
care being taken as to where they are made
fast on the pontoon.

If the yacht is coming in a bit fast then both
the bow and stern lines need, initially at least,
to be led to a cleat slightly aft of the eventual
position of the boat to act as short snubbing
springs. In this case it is vital that both
members of crew tending these lines
understand fully what is required. The plan
will be to put both bow and stern lines around
a cleat or bollard and slow the boat down by
applying friction.

If the lines are made fast while the yacht is
still going forward then the loads imposed on
cleats and ropes will be immense and there is
the real danger of damage. Also, if one end of
the yacht is brought to a halt quicker than the
other, that end will inevitably swing in hard
towards the pontoon while the other end will
be forced out. Thus, both lines will need to be
surged around their cleats evenly, whilst

watching how the yacht is responding and applying more or less friction as required.

All this means that a good briefing is essential before coming alongside otherwise the crew will be working in the dark and may not be as skilled as yourself at the manoeuvre and may therefore do the wrong thing. Make sure that each crew member has a task, understands the urgency or otherwise of that task and appreciates exactly which cleat you want the lines taken to and whether or not you want tension on the lines immediately.

While the warps should all end up with the ends ashore and the slack taken up onboard the yacht, it does not matter how they are put onto the cleats initially. Normally it is simplest for the crew to take relatively short lengths ashore with them, say from the cleat on the yacht to about amidships plus a little more. In this way there are not huge amounts of rope to get tangled.

If coming to a tidal-alongside berth, for example a harbour wall or similar, then the yacht will need to be tied up with long bow and stern lines and long springs otherwise they will need to be tended very frequently as the tide rises or falls. If the wind is blowing the yacht off the wall then it can often be worth

having a loose centre line with which the yacht can be pulled in close alongside when crew members want to get on or off her.

Other Yachts

If coming alongside another yacht which is already moored alongside, then the first priority is always to secure safely to the yacht, then worry about shore lines. Treat the other yacht virtually as if she were a pontoon and approach and tie up with breasts and springs in the usual way. The only difference is that your fenders will probably need to be quite a bit higher than for most pontoons.

Once secure alongside the other yacht, it is courteous to take lines from your bow and stern to the shore, pontoon or piles ensuring that they are led sensibly so as not to chafe. The ideal tension is that which just takes some of the load of your boat off the breast lines. If the lines are any tighter than this they will be holding the other yachts inshore as well as your own, any looser and they are not really going to do anything at all.

The reasons for putting out shore lines are twofold. Firstly, it takes some of the strain off the warps of the yacht(s) inside you. Secondly,

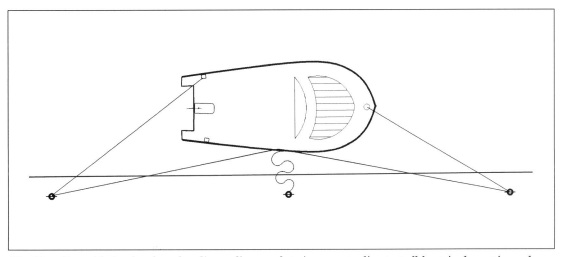

Fig 48   Alongside berth – long head/stern lines and springs, centre line to pull boat in for getting ashore.

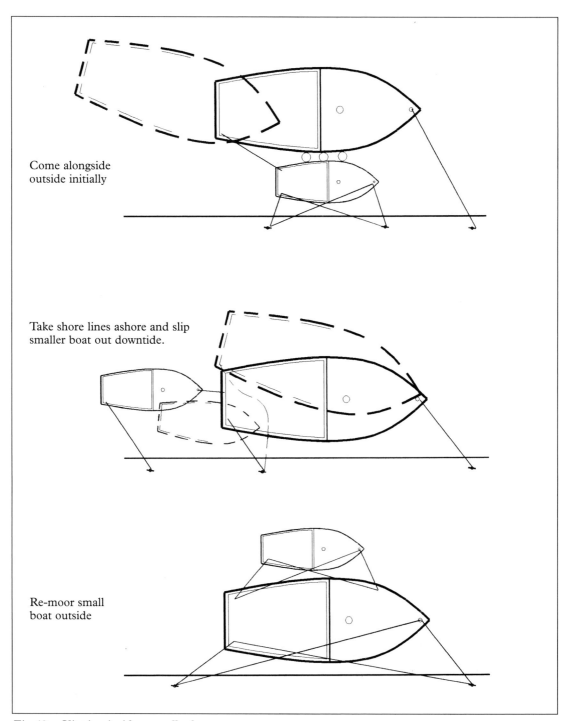

Come alongside
outside initially

Take shore lines ashore and slip
smaller boat out downtide.

Re-moor small
boat outside

Fig 49   Slipping inside a smaller boat.

it means that, should an inside boat wish to depart then they can do this without having to rummage around on your boat to find lines to tie you to the shore.

If coming alongside a berth where you have to lie outside another yacht then, whenever possible, you should aim to find one which is at least as big as your own yacht to tie to. If this is not possible and you are forced to come alongside a much smaller yacht, it is courteous and safe, especially with an onshore wind, to temporarily secure on the outside, then slip the smaller yacht(s) outside you so that you are taking the strain of them rather than vice versa.

If alongside a wall then it will often be necessary to rig a fender board to spread the load and stop the fenders from falling between uprights on the wall. Any length of wood will suffice and these are often provided by the harbour master.

A common mistake is to attach the board to the wall – then as the tide rises or falls it is left there totally useless. Even if it is chained loosely to the wall it should be tied onto your yacht at a suitable height for your fenders so that it goes up and down as she does.

When leaving, do not forget to untie the board from the yacht and tie it to the wall (unless it is yours and you are taking it away with you). It can be very embarrassing to start motoring away from a crowded harbour wall only to be arrested by the loose chains once you are a metre or two away!

Approaching into the Tide

This is the easiest way to approach any berth because as already mentioned, it allows a slower speed over the ground whilst maintaining steerage way and facilitates stopping.

You should try to judge your approach so that, if at all possible, you are coming at the berth either straight on or at a slight angle, maybe 10–20 degrees, pointing in towards the berth. If the wind is blowing you onto the berth and there is enough space then, as stated earlier, it is best to be aiming for a point some distance, perhaps a metre or so, off the berth. You can then stop level with your chosen position and allow the wind to blow you in alongside. If the wind is blowing you off, then a close approach will be necessary.

It is very hard to judge the exact beam of the yacht from most steering positions and help from the crew can be invaluable, especially for coping with this latter case. Always ensure that the boom and any other restrictions to your visibilty are moved to the side away from the pontoon to give you as good a view of your approach as possible.

If the wind is blowing you off very strongly it will be extremely difficult to put the yacht alongside and for the crew to step ashore with the lines before she is blown too far away for sensible disembarking. If faced with this it can often be easier and safer to temporarily moor to a downwind berth opposite the required pontoon and then warp the yacht across when secure.

If this is not possible then you are probably going to need to be quite aggressive with regard to boat speed on your approach in order to keep leeway to a minimum. You may also need to make your approach at a greater angle into the wind than normal and swing the yacht round at the last moment. If your prop-walk swings the stern in towards the berth then this is not quite as hard as it sounds but does obviously increase the risk of making a mistake and thus causing damage.

One of the mistakes often seen around marinas where the gaps between boats are very tight, is for a yacht to come in expecting to be able to squeeze through a small gap and continue unchecked to her own berth. This is particularly difficult if there is another yacht on the same pontoon as yours so that you first have to go through a gap and then turn sharply to get to your berth.

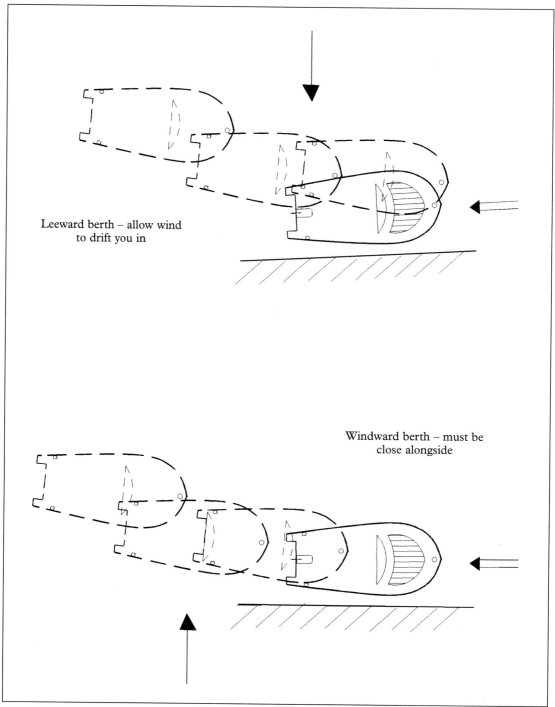

Leeward berth – allow wind
to drift you in

Windward berth – must be
close alongside

Fig 50   Coming alongside – leeway.

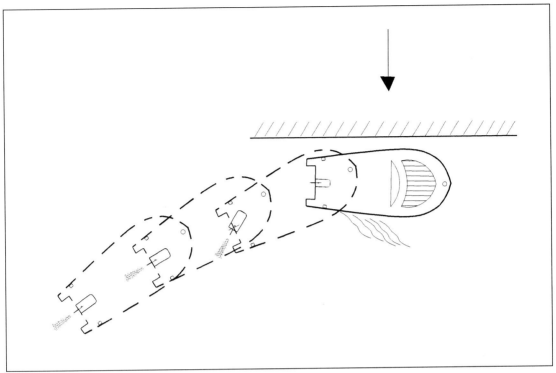

Fig 51   Coming alongside using propwalk when possible.

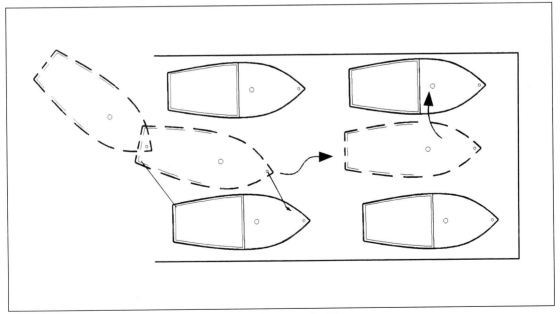

Fig 52   Difficult berth – use a temporary mooring to make life easy.

The safest option is often to plan initially to moor to whatever is on the downwind side of the narrow gap, with plenty of fenders on both sides. Then, once temporarily secure, warp the yacht forward and up into your proper berth. It may seem a trifle long-winded, but a few extra minutes spent doing this can easily mean the difference between a safe and calm mooring situation and a last minute panic with possible damage to both your own yacht and to those either side of the gap you are squeezing through.

Similarly, if your berth is at the end of a long pontoon with another yacht very close to you on the opposing side see if there is space at the outer end of the pontoon. If there is it is sensible to come alongside the clear pontoon first, then warp the yacht along to your berth.

If choosing a berth, then wherever possible give yourself a way out if things go wrong. Obviously an outside berth with nothing in front of you is the easiest of all since, if you do not like your final approach, it is possible to simply increase speed and motor around for another attempt. In all cases think about what might happen if, for example, the wind gusts up at just the wrong moment. Attempt to have plans to deal with all eventualities.

Approaching Downtide

This is a situation to be avoided whenever possible! If the tide is weak then life may not be too hard but if there is a strong tide under you as you approach the berth then it will be very difficult to maintain steerage-way without travelling dangerously fast over the ground. It will also be that much harder to stop when you get to your berth and if the wind is blowing you forwards then it gets even more difficult.

My advice in any berthing situation where the designated berth is downtide, is to consider carefully whether there are any alternative mooring places before committing yourself to what may well be a dangerous option. Possibly the tide will turn in a short while and you could moor temporarily on another berth until the tide has turned or possibly the harbour master could allocate you another berth for the night if you are just visiting.

If you are forced to come in downtide then you should try to make everything else as simple as possible. Downtide and being blown off by a strong wind adds two difficult situations together, probably making it well nigh impossible. Consider all the options such as coming temporarily onto a leeward berth and warping yourself across once secure, as described in the previous section.

Downtide, the most important mooring line is going to be a spring to stop you going too far forward. It is much safer if this comes from about the centre of the yacht rather than from the bow because the latter will almost certainly cause the bow to swing hard into the pontoon. The crew member handling the spring must understand how to surge the rope rather than snubbing it hard otherwise damage is almost bound to result.

The second most important line will be the stern line which will need to be attached, and surged as quickly as possible after the spring and ideally at the same time. The bow line and second spring are much less important and can usually wait until the initial adrenalin surge has died away!

In some berthing situations it may be possible to moor for a while to an uptide berth, possibly just by the bow, and then drop back into your own berth using a long warp on a slip from your temporary berth together with a long stern line to your pontoon. Alternatively, it may be feasible to anchor just uptide of your berth and then pay out cable until you reach your own berth. Anchoring in marinas is not usually a good idea however because of the likelihood of there being objects on the bottom to snag the anchor.

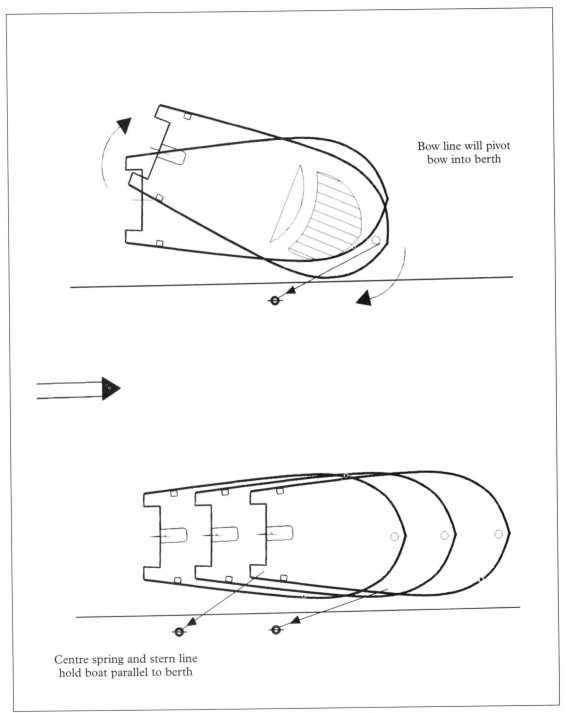

Bow line will pivot
bow into berth

Centre spring and stern line
hold boat parallel to berth

Fig 53   Coming alongside downtide – use centre spring and stern line.

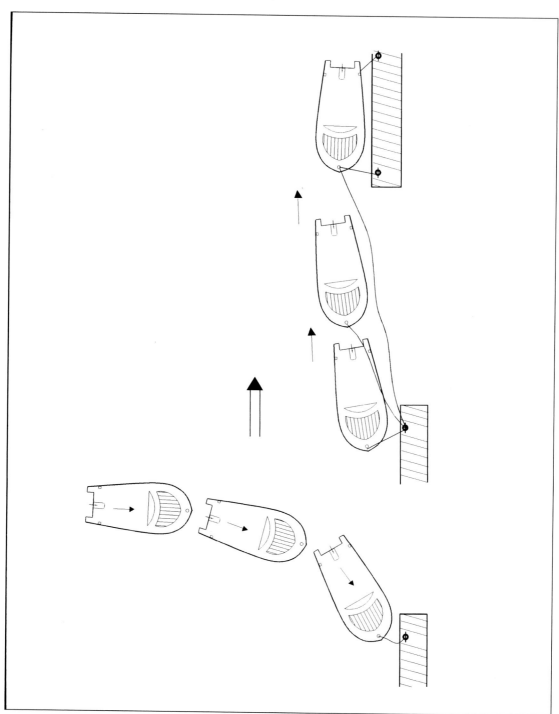

Fig 54 Coming alongside downtide – temporarily moor to upstream berth.

Leaving an Alongside Berth

Simple Situations

If the wind is not blowing your yacht onto the berth, or at least not too hard, then leaving should not normally present too many problems.

Consider which way the wind and current are trying to move the yacht and remove any lines which are not needed to hold her in place. If outside other yachts, this is usually the time to remove your shore lines. Once you have reduced the number of lines to a minimum, it is often worth rigging slip-ropes for the remainder so that you can slip away from the pontoon with all your crew on board.

Treat each situation individually. There is little point in going to the bother of rigging slip-ropes if there is no wind or current and you have enough sprightly crew to enable the last couple of lines to be untied from the shore. They can then give you a push from the pontoon before you motor away. My general plan in any leaving situation is to make it as simple as possible for all crew members.

In most situations, at least one spring will be redundant just before you come to leave and this can be removed and tidied away. Long head and stern ropes can be transferred so that they become short breast ropes. Any bow lines which might prove hard to untie at the last minute can be untied and either the lines re-rigged as slips or possibly retied with a couple of half hitches for a short time.

If any lines are really under strain, then it may be necessary to rig short slip-ropes taking the load in the same direction as the original ropes before slacking off and removing the lines which were under tension.

Springing Off

If there is another yacht or an obstruction to prevent you from motoring straight out from the berth then you will need to get the upstream end of the yacht pointing outwards.

This can either be done simply by getting a crew member to push that end of the yacht away from the pontoon or by 'springing off' – using a short, slippable spring attached to the downstream end of the yacht. By motoring against the spring the end of the yacht attached to the shore swings inwards and the other end pivots out.

Obviously you need to remember to move at least one fender to the end by the spring otherwise the yacht will pivot into the pontoon. It is often worth having another fender held by a crew member, ready to place wherever it may be needed.

Whether you leave forwards or backwards will depend on which way you are facing and on how well the yacht handles in astern. The important point to remember is that you must (nearly) always leave against the current.

Wind Blowing you onto the Pontoon

If the wind is blowing you onto the pontoon or wall then it will not be possible to simply push off and you will always need to spring off, even if there is no obstruction to miss. If you attempt to simply motor away without springing off, the yacht is bound to be pushed against the pontoon and scrape her way along it, possibly causing damage and certainly not being neat and safe.

There will be some situations where the wind is so strong and the yacht is pinned so hard against the lee shore that it is not feasible to spring off without the risk of damage. Here, the best option may be to find another pontoon or mooring to windward of your current berth, take a warp(s) to that and winch yourself off the lee shore. From there it should present no problems to leave since you will be blown away from the temporary mooring.

If there is nothing available to windward, it may be necessary to take an anchor out to windward in a dinghy, get that well dug in and then winch yourself out using the anchor. If doing this, the anchor will need to be taken at

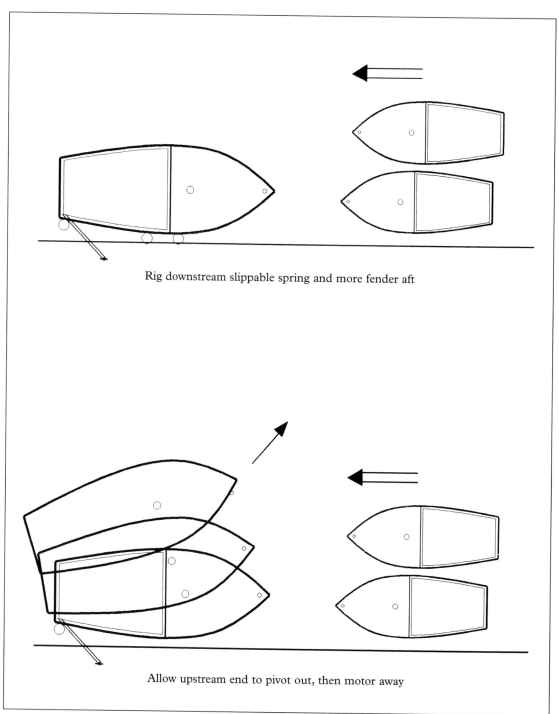

Rig downstream slippable spring and more fender aft

Allow upstream end to pivot out, then motor away

Fig 55   Springing off.

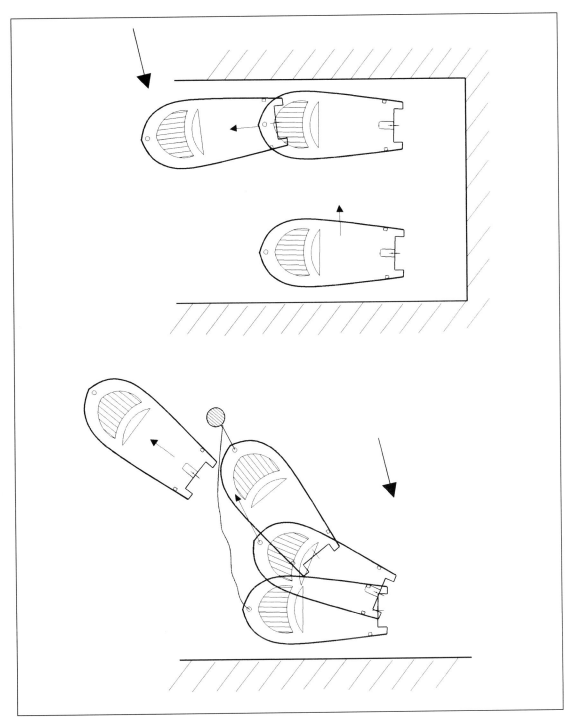

Fig 56   *Leaving a leeward berth – first move to windward berth if possible.*

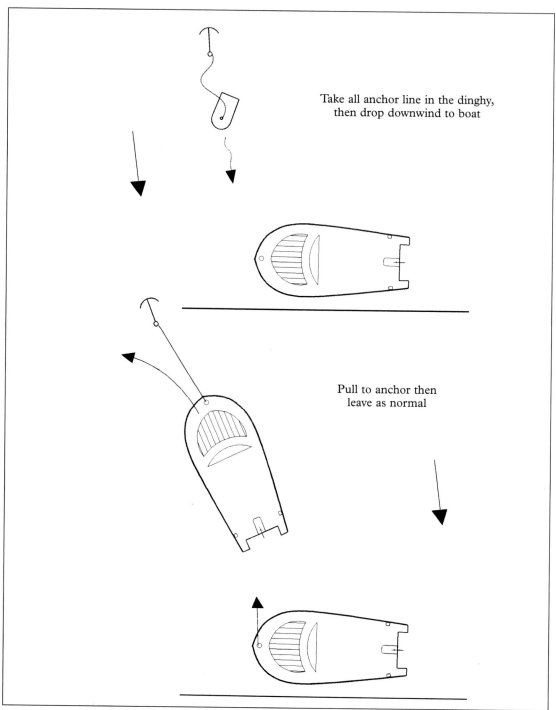

Take all anchor line in the dinghy,
then drop downwind to boat

Pull to anchor then
leave as normal

Fig 57   Leaving a leeward berth – row an anchor out.

least five or six boat lengths to windward before it is dropped otherwise as you start to winch yourself away from the pontoon the anchor will drag and you will drift back onto the lee shore.

If there are Boats Outside

If lying on a harbour wall, you will often find yourself in the situation that, when you want to leave there are other yachts moored outside you. In my experience there is never anyone on the other yachts when you want to leave and wind and tide usually contrive to make life as difficult as possible.

The are three ways that can be used to extricate yourself from an inside berth. By far the easiest for the yacht leaving is for the boat(s) lying outside her to motor off, let the inside yacht leave, and then return to their moorings. However it is quite rare to find other crews who are willing to go to this bother. Having said that, the rights are always with the inside yacht and if conditions are particularly tough, it may be worth insisting that the outside yachts go in order to let you out. If the outside yachts do temporarily leave then getting away is exactly the same as if they had never been there.

If you are left with yachts outside you when you need to leave then you can either move them to an adjacent berth, or slip out from inside them, leaving them effectively in the same place. Given the choice and space, it is nearly always easier to move the other yachts to another berth, especially if they do not have any crew members on board to help.

If you are able to move the other yachts, use warps and be very careful not to lose them in a strong tide or wind. Always have lines ashore before casting off their lines from your boat and be aware that if you are moving them without a responsible member of their own crew in charge, you may be liable for any damage caused to them.

Finally we get to the situation where you have to slip out from inside another yacht. A shore line must be taken from the upstream end of the outside yacht to stop the yacht being swept out into the current. A second shore line is then taken from the downstream end, around the outside of your own vessel and onto the shore (or other vessel inside) to act as a temporary spring. You then cast off all your own lines, and motor/manhandle your yacht out downtide.

If there are crew on-board the outside vessel, it should be all right to leave them to pull themselves in and secure properly. However, if there is no one on-board at the time you are slipping out then it will be necessary to temporarily leave one or more of your own crew on her to tend the lines.

This is one of the few times when it is necessary to leave downtide. If you attempted to leave in an uptide direction, it would be virtually impossible to prevent the outside yacht from being swept away and, while it might well be easier for yourself, you would leave carnage behind!

If there is nothing directly behind you this procedure should not present any real difficulties. However, if, as is often the case, there is another row of yachts moored directly downstream of your own trot, then the whole operation is likely to become quite messy, with your crew having to hand your yacht around to the outside of the downstream trot.

SWINGING SHIP USING WARPS

While on Piles

Swinging ship or 'winding' the yacht around always looks impressive when done well but can also give onlookers a lot of fun when it is not done properly. As with most other manoeuvres, the secrets of success lie in making it as simple as possible and in letting the

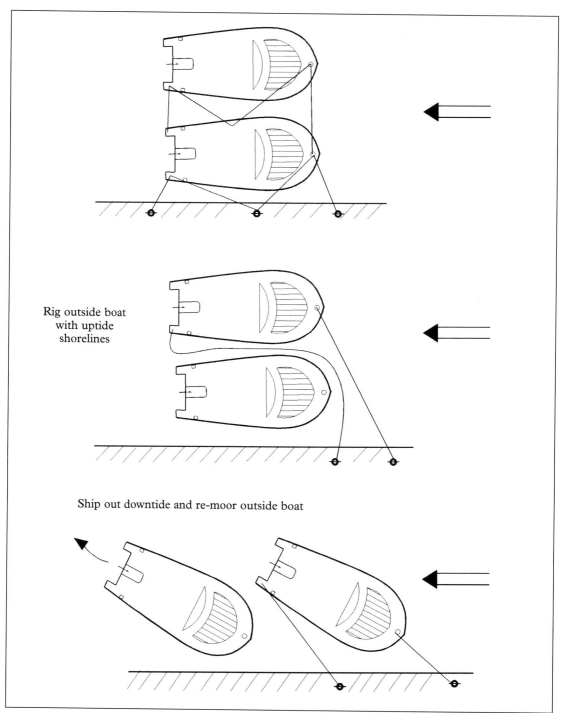

Rig outside boat
with uptide
shorelines

Ship out downtide and re-moor outside boat

Fig 58   Shipping out from an inside berth.

natural forces of the wind and current do most of the work for you.

The two most common mistakes are to use an excessive number of warps and thus complicate the manoeuvre or to attempt to turn the yacht against the prevailing conditions – with the inevitable result.

There are many reasons why it may be necessary or desirable to swing the yacht around. Sometimes, the easiest solution will be to motor off and then return facing the other way but this is not always the case. For example, it may be that you are currently facing the tide but are going to want to leave after the tide has turned and do not, for some reason, want to go out backwards. This will mean that before leaving your berth you will need to turn the yacht around.

Another possible time when swinging ship is useful is when you find yourself lying with your stern to the wind and rain, with water finding its way down below. Once again, the easy answer is to turn the yacht around.

The simplest time to swing the yacht right around is when on a pair of piles and so we will look at this situation first. To make understanding the principles as simple as possible, we will deal with a situation where there is no current and the day is calm. We will then look at the differences as current and wind are added into the equation.

Flat Water

Imagine your yacht, moored between two piles with single head and stern ropes tied with bowlines. This is where you need to start. To

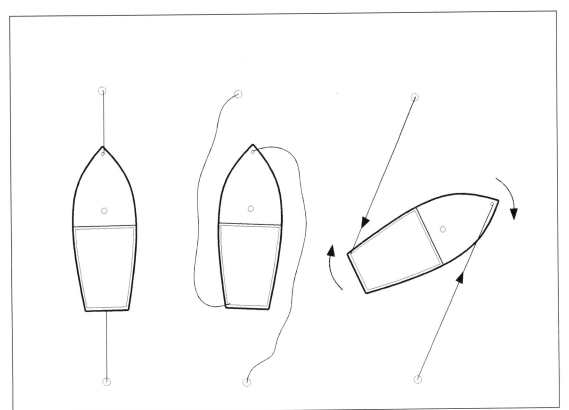

Fig 59   Winding ship on piles

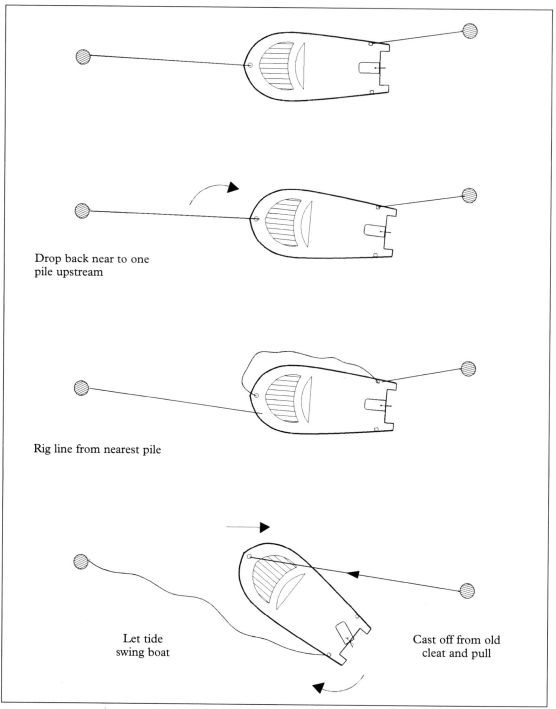

Drop back near to one
pile upstream

Rig line from nearest pile

Let tide
swing boat

Cast off from old
cleat and pull

Fig 60   Winding ship on piles.

swing the yacht you will need to transfer the old bow line, down one side to the stern and at the same time transfer the old stern line down the other side to the bow. Pulling on both ropes will then force the yacht to pivot around her keel until she is facing the other way. She can then be centred up between the piles and resecured. In this situation, no extra ropes are required – all you need for success is enough room to either side for the yacht to swing around unhindered.

Swinging in a Current

Next let us look at a situation, virtually as before but this time with tide or current running along the yacht. The principle will still be exactly the same but there is now a real danger that the yacht will hit the downtide pile as she turns and steps must be taken to counteract this tendency.

In most cases, it will be sufficient to move the yacht as close to the uptide pile as possible before commencing the swing and then carry on exactly as before. The thing to remember is that it will be the line from the uptide pile which will end up taking all the load and this must be handled with care and the crew must be ready to heave or winch this in if the yacht drifts too far downtide during the swing. The line from the downtide pile will end up slack (or virtually so) and can be entrusted to any crew member who can just be told to hold onto it and walk gently from one end of the yacht to the other!

In order to ensure that the uptide line is ready, the end of it should be taken out through the fairlead and then outside everything to a cleat or winch at the other end of the yacht, before it is cast off from its cleat. Then, once the crew are ready, this line can be let go from its old cleat and rapidly pulled in. Assuming there is no wind to help blow the boat around, it will help considerably to put the helm over to initiate the swing in the right direction.

If the current is very strong, it is also a wise precaution to have the engine ticking over in neutral so that you are able to motor back towards the uptide pile and take some load off the rope if this becomes necessary. It is also a good idea to move the yacht fairly close to the upstream pile before commencing the manoeuvre since this gives you most swinging room and entails the least amount of pulling while you are in a vulnerable position during the swing.

Swinging in a Wind

Finally let us add some wind into the equation. This does not really alter the principles at all except to make one direction of swing easy

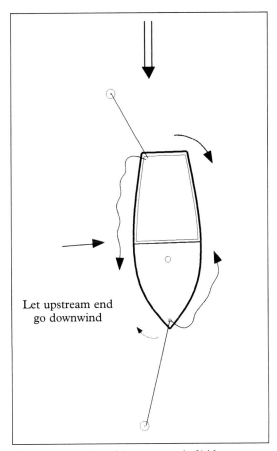

Let upstream end
go downwind

Fig 61   Winding ship – cross wind/tide.

and the other almost impossible. Remember that most yachts will turn their bows downwind if left to their own devices and this gives you the information as to which way to swing the yacht around if there is no tide.

The bow should be allowed to swing off downwind and thus the lines need to be arranged on the correct sides to allow this to happen – that is with the line which was attached to the bow on the windward side and the line which was on the stern to leeward.

In other respects the manoeuvre is carried out exactly the same as before. The only additional point to remember is that the yacht will tend to lie outside the direct line between the piles as she is being blown sideways and thus may take more room to swing than before. If room is tight then both lines may need to be tended a bit sharper and with more care than if there is no wind to worry about.

If there is tide as well as wind then it will normally be the uptide end of the yacht which should be allowed to swing to leeward.

From an Alongside Berth

If lying alongside a pontoon, quay or another yacht then the basic principles of swinging the yacht are still exactly the same. If there is no wind or tide then it does not matter which way the yacht is swung. In this simple case, take off the springs and any other ropes apart from one head and one stern rope.

If swinging so that the stern goes out and the bow in, transfer the bow line onto the outboard cleat and fairlead, leading it around the bow and back to the shore. This means that it will be on the correct, inboard side once you have swung the yacht. Next take an extra long rope, from the outboard fairlead at the stern, outside all guard rails and shrouds, right around the yacht and onto the shore at the bow. This will become the stern line once the yacht has been swung around. Next transfer at least half the fenders to the other side, leaving one free as a safety fender.

Finally all you have to do is cast off the old stern line and walk the bow line (and bow of the yacht) backwards along the pontoon while pushing the stern out. Once she starts to move, it will be possible to pull gently on the new stern line to pivot the yacht around.

In this no wind, no tide situation, the only possible danger is that of the bow being pulled in towards the pontoon (or other yacht) and causing damage. As long as a crew member is there to push and/or fend off and the person on the stern line does not pull it too hard this should not really be any problem.

If there is current flowing along the yacht then this actually makes the whole process even easier. In this case though, you have no choice as to which way to swing – the uptide end of the yacht *must* be swung out. The preparation is virtually the same as before except that, now there is current flowing, the spring from the yacht's downtide end will be under tension and thus cannot simply be let go.

The best plan is to arrange a 'spring' from the downtide end of your yacht, outside everything to a position on the pontoon a little further upstream than the yacht. This will become the new upstream breast rope once the yacht has been swung. Another long rope should be taken from the outboard side of the upstream end of the yacht, outside everything and around her outboard side. Eventually it should be brought back onto the pontoon in such a position that it will end up being both a downstream breast rope and short spring.

The downstream breast rope should be released first. The upstream breast is then let go and at the same time the yacht is steered out from the pontoon, using the tide to help. As with swinging the yacht on piles, it is now important to pull quite hard on the upstream line in order to get the yacht repositioned where she was before. The earlier in the turn that this pulling is done, the easier it will be. If the tide is very strong it may be worth

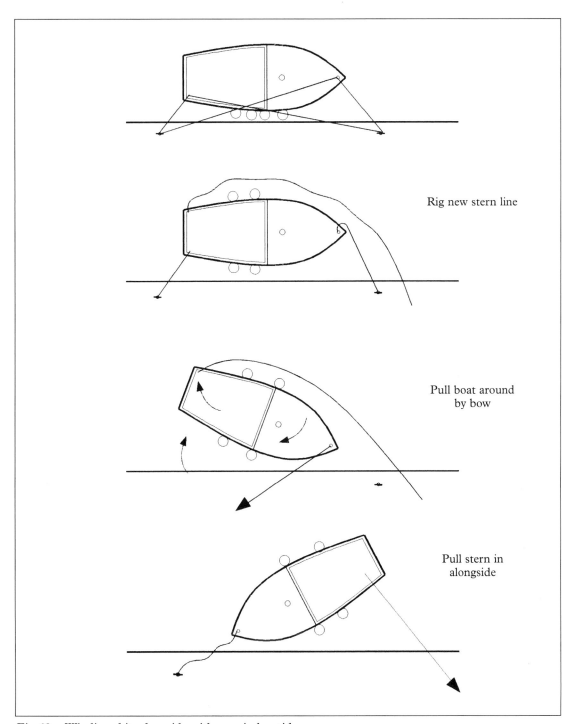

Rig new stern line

Pull boat around
by bow

Pull stern in
alongside

Fig 62   Winding ship alongside with no wind or tide.

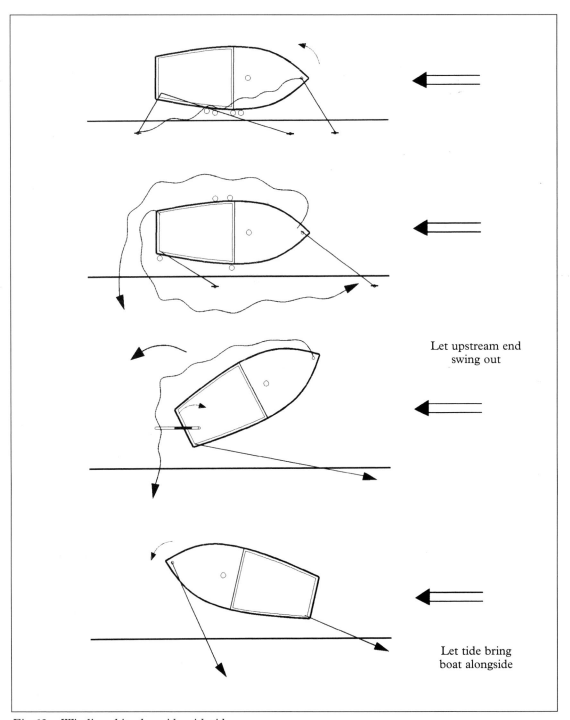

Let upstream end
swing out

Let tide bring
boat alongside

Fig 63   Winding ship alongside with tide.

motoring uptide slightly in the early stages of the turn.

As the yacht goes beam onto the tide it will seem as if she is turning much too fast and it will look as if she is going to swing in and smash against the pontoon. In fact however, the rate of swing will slow as soon as she is past that point and she should swing gently back alongside the pontoon.

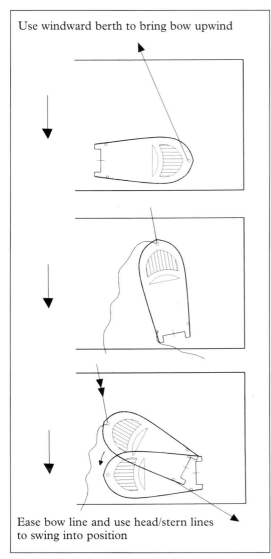

Use windward berth to bring bow upwind

Ease bow line and use head/stern lines to swing into position

Fig 64   Winding ship from a leeward berth.

With an Onshore Wind

If there is a strong onshore wind then it is often best not to attempt to swing the yacht from an alongside situation because there will be the real danger of the yacht being blown onto the pontoon harder than it is possible to fend her off.

However, it is still possible to swing the yacht if there is an upwind pontoon available temporarily. Simply warp the yacht over to the upwind pontoon, then swing her around in the space between the two pontoons and finally warp her back to her proper pontoon. Even simpler might be to only warp one end up to the upwind pontoon at a time, swinging the vessel in the process.

ANCHORING

So far as the basic boat handling is concerned, anchoring is virtually identical to picking up a swinging mooring. Positioning is not quite so critical although an understanding of how the yacht will lie and swing to her anchor is essential.

To anchor with all chain (of a suitable size) in normal conditions, you need a length of cable of about three times the maximum depth of the water. If using a majority of warp with just a few metres of chain at the end, you will need about five times the depth. Both these figures are very approximate and depend heavily on what sort of 'bottom' you are anchoring in; how strong the wind and tide are expected to become and the type, weight and windage of your yacht. Even just anchoring for a short stay, you will need a length at least three times the depth of the water if using chain and warp together.

When kedging in open water, perhaps in quite a great depth, it is important to have a kedge line that is not too thick. This is because the usual reason for kedging is to wait in calm conditions for the turn of the tide. You will find that if the warp is too thick, you need disproportionately more warp and a heavier anchor to hold you because the tidal drag on the warp itself becomes the greatest factor affecting your holding power.

Racing in the English Channel it is quite common to need to kedge in up to 100 metres of water – it is not hard to see that this needs at least 300–400 metres of line and that if this is any thicker than it needs to be, you have little chance of getting the anchor to hold.

Selecting an Anchorage

If coming into an anchorage, look at the chart or pilot book before getting there to ascertain depths, type of bottom, any dangers and places to land. This should give you a reasonable mental picture of the anchorage which will help in deciding where to drop your hook.

When you arrive, sail or motor around first to look at any other anchored or moored boats and see how they are lying. This should give you an idea of the direction of any current and also, of where gaps may be between the existing boats.

The amount of room required for swinging to your anchor as the wind or tide changes will obviously depend on both the depth of water and on whether you are using all chain or a combination of chain and warp. However, as long as you are anchoring amongst other boats of a generally similar type to your own, they should swing in the same sort of way.

In a really crowded anchorage, it is usually possible to find a safe place to be anchored while the current is holding all yachts in the same way. However bear in mind that it is at the turn of the tide, when anchored boats will be lying all over the place, that problems might occur.

Once you have selected your anchoring spot, you need to decide how to approach it. As stated before, if there are other yachts

already at anchor then the way they are lying is probably the right way to approach your spot. Motor up to the place where you intend to drop the anchor and slow down as you get closer. Just before your crew let the anchor go, stop completely (over the ground) checking that you are not making forward way by looking at right angles to your vessel at the shore or near objects.

If there are no other vessels already at anchor, you must make a decision as to which way the wind and tide are going and as to how you will end up lying. If in doubt, come to your anchorage against the tide, or if there is no appreciable tide, against the wind.

When the crew lower the anchor away make sure that enough cable is released so that the anchor is firmly on the seabed but not so much that the cable might lie on top of the anchor and get tangled up. Motor gently backwards away from the anchor with the crew letting out more cable as you go. Prior to letting go, you should have already decided how much cable you want out and this should be prepared on the foredeck. Once all the cable has been let out you should give the engine a good burst astern to bite the anchor into the seabed and to check that it is holding.

Once again, look at right angles to the vessel, taking either a transit with fixed objects or a bearing to a single fixed object to check you are not dragging the anchor. Another check is for one of your crew to feel the anchor cable as it comes over the bow roller while you are digging the anchor in. If the anchor is holding, the cable will go taut whereas if it is dragging there might be some slack or, more probably, you will be able to feel a juddering in the line as the anchor drags over (or through) the seabed.

Once you are happy that the anchor has held securely, it is always a good idea to hoist an anchor ball – a black spherical shape of suitable size for your yacht – in the fore part of the rigging. At night, it is sensible to display an

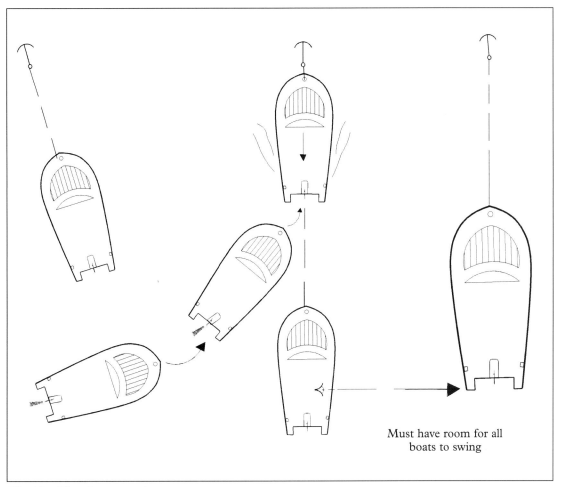

Must have room for all
boats to swing

Fig 65   Choosing an anchorage.

all round white light as an anchor light although obviously these precautions are not necessary in totally isolated anchorages.

If the anchor refuses to bite properly, the simplest option is often to raise it and try again. It is possible that it has got some seaweed or part of the cable wrapped around it or you might simply be trying to anchor on a flat piece of rock.

If you are anchoring in an area where there might be old mooring chains or other obstructions on the seabed, or if it is a rocky area, it can be a good idea to use a tripping line to ensure the anchor can be raised when required. This should be fastened to the crown of the anchor and either taken back on board with slack between you and the anchor or alternatively, be tied to a fender or small buoy and allowed to float above the anchor.

When cruising, I like to have a small buoy with a pickup handle ready with the words 'anchor buoy' or similar written on it. This helps to prevent a later arrival from picking up your trip line thinking it is a mooring!

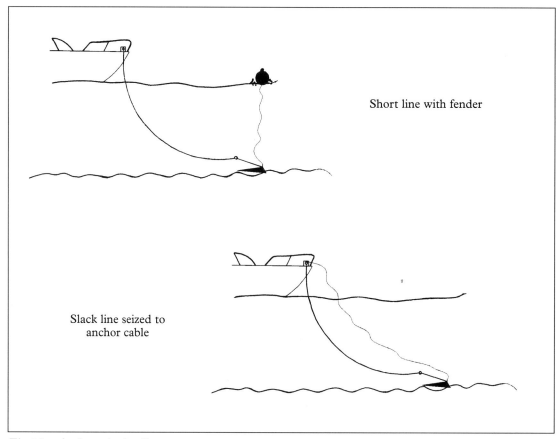

Short line with fender

Slack line seized to
anchor cable

Fig 66   Anchor tripping lines.

Weighing Anchor

Weighing anchor under power should be relatively simple, even if hard work unless you have a power windlass. Motor gently up toward the anchor, following the direction given by the anchor cable, with one or more crew members pulling in the slack as you go. Once virtually above the anchor, the cable is bound to go tight and if being pulled in by hand will almost certainly need to be snubbed on a cleat. The momentum of the yacht can then be used to break the anchor free from the seabed, motoring ahead as hard as necessary.

Obviously if you used a trip line, this can be used to haul the anchor upside down off the bottom. Once the anchor has broken free, way should be taken off the yacht while the rest of the cable is pulled in, otherwise there is a real danger that you will end up with the anchor and/or cable damaging the hull, keel or topsides as you drag it through the water. Get you crew to signal as soon as the anchor is clear of the surface and off you go.

Standard terminology is useful in these circumstances since it ensures that both you and your foredeck crew understand each other. Simple hand signals are the easiest way for the crew to let you know which way to steer, followed by a call of 'up and down' when you get directly over the anchor and 'clear' once it is out of the water and it is safe for you to go ahead.

If it is too windy for voices to carry aft, a beckoning motion with the hand should be used to mean 'continue coming forward', a clenched fist to mean 'stop', a vertical raising and lowering of an arm to mean the anchor is up and down and a thumbs up to indicate that it is clear of the surface.

STERN-TO (MEDITERRANEAN) MOORINGS

Mooring stern (or bow) onto a pontoon or jetty is the norm in the Mediterranean even though it is fairly unusual in the UK. Some stern-to jetties will have a row of buoys anchored off the jetty to act as bow moorings, if this is not the case then an anchor will have to be laid to hold the bow in position and to stop the yacht from hitting the jetty.

This system of mooring is used wherever there is little tidal rise and fall and where there is no marina, since it allows for a far higher density of yachts than is possible using other methods, such as lying two or three abreast alongside the same jetty. Assuming the average yacht is three times as long as it is wide, mooring stern-to automatically gives one the equivalent of lying three deep and because yachts can be moored right next to each other with no space in between, it probably gives an effective capacity of at least four or five deep. Added to this the advantage that any yacht can come or go with equal ease and it is not difficult to see why it so popular. It is not used where there is any flow of tide along the wall

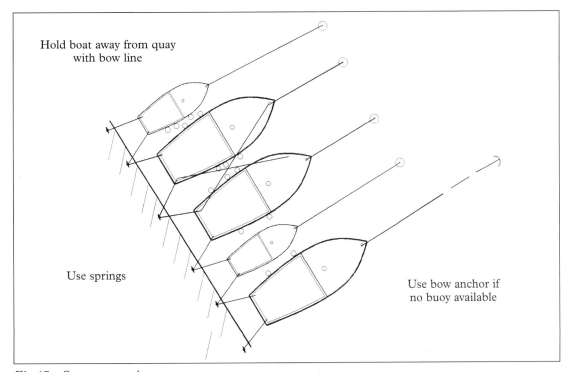

Fig 67 Stern-to mooring.

or jetty because this would make it virtually impossible to have yachts lying at right angles to the current.

Assuming there are mooring buoys offshore from the wall the general principles involved are quite straightforward. You need to have a longish bow warp prepared on the side that the buoy will be passed and also two stern lines ready. The yacht then needs to be positioned so that she can be driven straight in towards the wall, normally in reverse.

As the mooring buoy is passed, the bow line needs to be attached. If it is very windy or you are handling a large yacht, you might well need assistance for this part of the manoeuvre, either a local dock master in a semi-inflatable or one of your crew members in your own dinghy.

Once the bow line is secure, the yacht continues in towards the wall with enough speed to give steerage-way and to stop the bow falling off. The bow line should be kept slack until nearly at the wall when it can be used both as a brake and to keep the bow in position while the stern lines are secured ashore. The bow line should be tied to the buoy using a bowline with a large loop so that when you come to leave it is easy to untie.

If you end up alongside another yacht or even between two yachts, I prefer to rig springs to stop the yacht I am on from surging up and down the sides of the other yachts. However, this does make small adjustments to bow and stern ropes difficult for everyone since no one yacht is then able to move independently of the others. For this reason, it is quite common to see a whole jetty full of yachts moored just with the bow and stern lines and with nothing tied between each other.

When you go into a new port, look at how the other yachts are moored to give you an idea of what is acceptable locally. However, in the absence of any data to the contrary, rig springs as soon as you are secure.

If on a lee shore, remember that the only thing stopping your yacht from grinding her stern into the wall is your bow line. This not only has to be tight enough to stop the yacht from falling back even in the biggest gusts but it, and its mooring, must be strong enough. If conditions are severe, it is always more

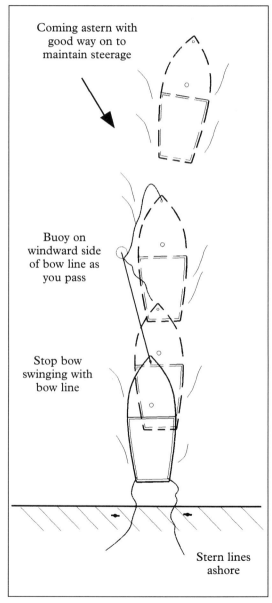

Fig 68   *Approaching a stern-to berth.*

comfortable to be lying to two moorings rather than one and at least to two lines from the bow, even if they both have to go to the same mooring.

Once secure, in most situations you will need a gang plank to enable the crew to get ashore without the need for athletic leaps. While in very calm conditions, this can be a simple plank, laid on the top of the transom and on the dockside. However, this is not the safest system if there is any chance of the yacht surging even a little, in and out from the wall.

In most cases it is better to fasten the inboard end of the 'plank' to the yacht and have the shore end suspended from the main halyard such that it is a few centimetres above the dockside. This allows the yacht to move around without the danger of the plank doing damage.

If the berth is a lee shore as you approach and it is very windy, you might well decide that going in stern first is simply too hard and potentially too dangerous. Reversing in with the wind on or near the bow is always going to be tricky since the bow is going to tend to pay off downwind and you will have to keep more power and speed on than you might feel really comfortable.

In such a situation do not hesitate to go in forwards instead. Agreed it will be a little harder for your crew to get ashore but this is a small price to pay for the ability to get to the berth safely. Similarly, if handling a large yacht, do not be shy of asking the locals for assistance in getting your bow line onto the offshore mooring, or if necessary of standing off for a bit while you get your own dinghy launched.

Using an Anchor

If there are no offshore mooring buoys for you to attach your bow line to, or the wind is blowing hard onshore and you are unhappy about your ability to stop your yacht swinging as you go in, it will be necessary to drop an anchor directly offshore from your selected berth. You can then motor in backwards, paying out anchor cable as you go.

If using the anchor merely to hold the bow into the wind as you manoeuvre, it should not be necessary to let go too much cable. The anchor only needs to be lowered until it is on the seabed and then allowed to drag, with the tension on the anchor cable keeping the yacht at right angles to the wall. On the other hand, if you are going to be using your anchor to secure the bow once moored, it will need to be dropped far enough away from the wall so that you have a length of cable at least three times the depth of water (if using chain), or five times (if using chain and rope).

If you are using your anchor and there are already other vessels moored to the wall, remember that they too might have anchors down so be careful not to foul one of these. This is one of the times when it is probably sensible to have a short trip line attached to the anchor with a small buoy marking its position since this will allow later arrivals to see where your anchor is and thus avoid it.

The only downside of having an anchor buoy is that it does give other yachts a further hazard to avoid as they approach the mooring. Once again, look at what seems to be local custom if at all possible and follow the same rules as others are using.

Leaving a Stern-To Mooring

In most situations leaving a Mediterranean type of stern-to mooring under power is simplicity itself because you are almost bound to be able to motor out in forward gear directly away from any dangers.

The first bit of preparation is to remove any lines securing your yacht to those on either side of you. Then rig either one or perhaps both stern lines as slip-ropes (unless there is someone on shore who can simply let them go when required). Warm the engine up as usual and then slip the stern and motor out, taking in the slack in the bow line as you go and untying the warp as you get to the knot.

If just going out for a few hours it may well be worth leaving your dinghy tied to the buoy with the bow line coiled up inside. This makes it much easier when you return.

4

MOORING AND
BERTHING UNDER SAIL

This section looks in detail at the types of manoeuvre you are likely to carry out in harbour, such as picking up moorings and coming alongside while under sail.

Sailing within the confines of a harbour can be good fun or it can end up as unseamanlike and dangerous. The difference between these two possible outcomes lies chiefly in preparation but also in the experience of the skipper and, to a lesser extent, of the crew.

Weather conditions also play a part, with a manoeuvre which seemed perfectly safe when carried out in a gentle force three turning into a nightmare in a gusty force seven. Before putting your yacht and other people's property at risk by going into a situation with which you are unable to cope, it always makes sense to practice in relatively open waters and in conditions where you are confident of your abilities.

Preparation means thinking ahead, knowing the principles of what you are intending to do and organizing yourself, your crew and your yacht so that the manoeuvre can be carried out safely and efficiently. For example, if you might need to tack within a busy harbour ensure that your sailplan is suitable. Running in under a headsail alone might be simple enough but it may not give you the upwind manoeuvrability you require if you need to turn and face the wind. Simply getting warps

and fenders ready in plenty of time is another example of thinking ahead.

Let us now look at the individual mooring situations.

MOORING

Sailing onto a Mooring

In reasonable weather, sailing onto a swinging mooring should present no real problem. The important things to remember are first and foremost that you need a way out if your approach goes wrong and secondly that you must be able to de-power the sail(s) completely once the buoy has been picked up.

Planning your Approach
Planning your approach so that you have a way out will depend very much on the individual situation. If you have a choice of buoys to go for then this should not be too hard but if forced to go for a particular buoy then it may present more difficulties.

Try to ensure that wind and/or tide will take you away from the buoy if you are going too fast, drifting down onto the buoy may sound easier but once you have buoy or lines under the boat there is more than an even chance that something will get wrapped around the keel, rudder or propeller.

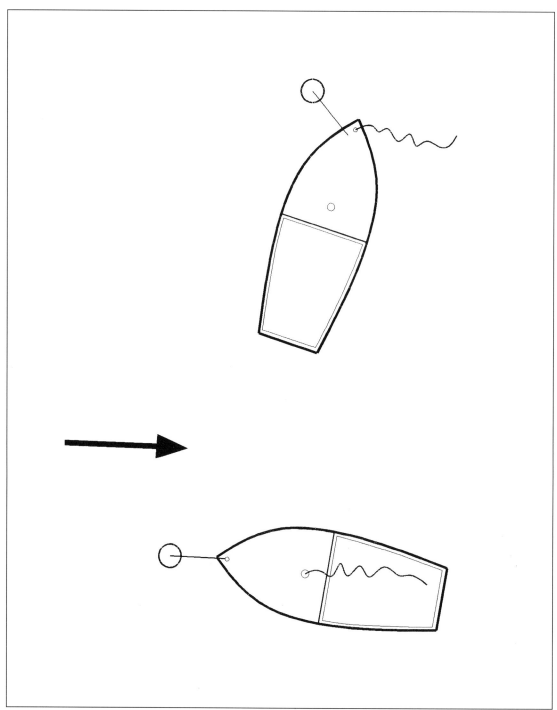

Fig 69   Main up if it will flap, down if unsure.

If possible, plan your approach so that, in the event of getting it wrong, you can just sheet-in and carry on in the same direction. Remember that if you have slowed down the yacht will make more leeway than usual as she picks up way again. If you should have to alter course significantly to avoid another yacht or the shore then have this in mind and be prepared to trim the sails accordingly – the yacht is unlikely to bear away with the main in and no jib set, for example.

As a general principle, the less sail you have set as you actually pick the buoy up, the easier the pick-up will be. However, if you have too little sail you might not have adequate control or steerage-way. If wind and tide are such that, once secured to the buoy, the mainsail will definitely flap, it is usually best to approach the buoy with the headsail down. This makes life on the foredeck much safer and enables clear communication to pass between bow crew and helmsman without the noise of a flapping headsail. However, if there is any chance that the mainsail will not flap because the wind is going to end up on or aft of the beam, then the mainsail *must* be dropped before you secure to the buoy.

The crew on the foredeck need to know how you plan to approach the buoy, which side of the bow you intend to put it, and how you and they are going to communicate as the buoy is approached. A system of hand signals for relaying the distance between the boat and the mooring saves a lot of shouting. A similar method is very useful for the crew to inform you of the buoy's position when it is under the bow.

You can tell whether the wind and tide are with or against each other by looking around you in the vicinity of your chosen mooring. If there are other yachts, preferably similar to your own, already on nearby moorings then the direction they are lying should give the best indication.

If all the yachts are lying head to wind (or nearly so) then it is a fair bet that there is either little tide or whatever tide there is will be going with the wind. If on the other hand, most yachts are lying with their sterns to the wind then it is fairly certain that the wind and tide are in opposition. If, as is often the case, the other yachts are lying stern to the wind but are being driven over their moorings by it, then the wind must be at least partly counteracting the tide and you know that it will be difficult to stop when you reach the buoy.

If there are no other yachts already on nearby moorings then you have to use other indicators. To start with, it is useful to have an idea of what you think the predicted tide should be doing before you even approach the mooring area.

It is a good idea to look at the tide tables for the port and compare your estimated time of arrival with high or low water. Then, if necessary, look at the local tidal stream atlas or tidal diamonds on the chart to confirm which way the tide should be flowing. Remember however, that tidal streams in river mouths or close to the shore do not always follow the most likely pattern and may well change direction several hours either side of the high or low water time.

It is nearly always a good idea to have a dummy run past your chosen mooring, unless the mooring area is very congested. This enables you to look at the buoy itself, decide how you are going to tie to it and also to look at the tidal stream. Even if the tide is weak you should be able to see ripples going off downtide or possibly seaweed on the mooring wafting downtide.

Wind Only (No Tide)
Assuming that the buoy is in clear water so that it can be approached from any angle, then this is probably the simplest of all situations. Unless the wind is very light, the approach should be made with just the mainsail. This

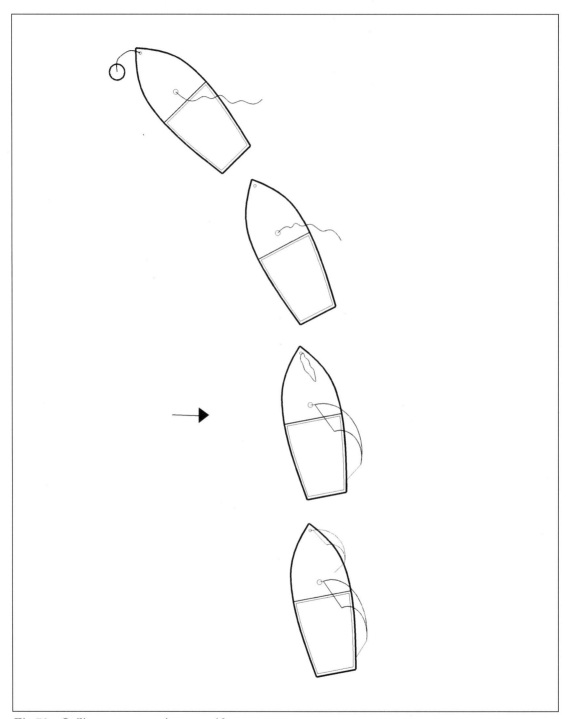

Fig 70   Sailing onto a mooring – no tide.

will be safe because, once secured to the mooring, the yacht will lie head to wind and the mainsail will therefore flap quite happily. Getting rid of the headsail will, as explained above, clear the foredeck, reduce the power in the sails and generally make life easier.

The simplest approach, needing least judgement will be to come towards the buoy on a close reach, with the wind at about 60 degrees to the bow. As the buoy is approached, way can be reduced by letting go of the mainsheet and spilling wind, so that once at the buoy, the yacht is virtually stationary. Make sure that the kicking strap (boom vang) is released before you make your final approach because with the kicker on, the leech of the mainsail will continue driving even when the sheet is eased off.

Unlike a man-overboard recovery, the buoy should be positioned to windward of the bow, then in the event of overshooting it, you can simply sheet-in and sail away. On most yachts, the foredeck crew will find it easiest if the

yacht is stopped with the buoy a metre or two back from the stem – but make sure they know this is your intention.

If the buoy has a pick-up line or a small pick-up buoy attached to it, then a boat-hook can be used to pull this onto the boat. Otherwise, the simplest and most certain method of fastening temporarily to the buoy will be to drop a loop of rope around the buoy.

One end of a warp should be made fast forward with the rest of the coil (say 5–6 metres) out through the windward bow fairlead. As the yacht stops by the buoy, a bight of this rope can be dropped or thrown over the buoy like a lasso and once the rope has sunk around the buoy's line, the other end can be secured forward. Once the yacht is secure, a proper mooring line should be attached to the buoy as appropriate.

Alternative Method

In really windy conditions, the yacht may not want to stop moving forward when on a reach

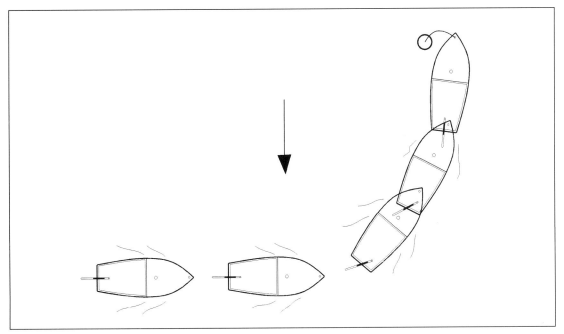

Fig 71 Sailing onto a mooring – no tide and windy.

even with the sails fully eased and here a different approach must be made.

Most of the preparations will be same as before but this time, the yacht should be sailed on a close reach to a point one or two boat lengths downwind of the buoy and then turned head to wind for the final approach. This method can be used at any time but it is inherently more difficult than the controlled close reach approach because you have to judge accurately the amount of way that the yacht will carry once head-to-wind. Turn too close to the buoy and you will overshoot, too far away and you will lose way and steerage before the buoy is reached and have to fall off, regain control and start again.

Easily driven hulls such as a modern racing yacht will have more tendency to keep moving with the sails flapping than would a heavy displacement, large wetted surface cruiser type of hull. However, they have the advantage that, due to their lighter weight, they will also lose speed faster when head-to-wind, thus making the judgement of where to aim for in your approach and when to turn into the wind less of a problem.

Wind With Tide

If the wind and tide are both in the same direction then sailing up to a swinging mooring should not be any more difficult than if there was no tide at all. It will be rare for the tide to be flowing in exactly the same direction as the wind is blowing and in most cases this discrepancy in directions will limit the approach to one tack only. In this situation the plan is to finish up alongside the buoy, with the buoy to windward as before, in more or

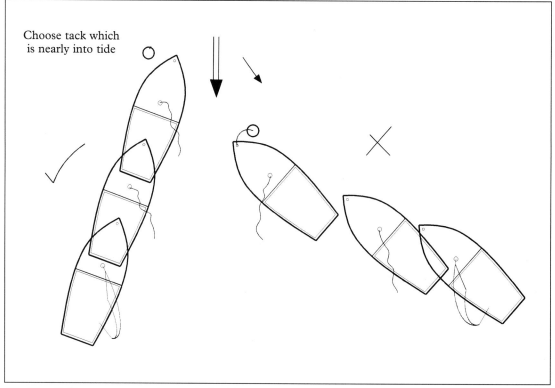

Fig 72   Sailing onto a mooring – wind with tide and choice of tack.

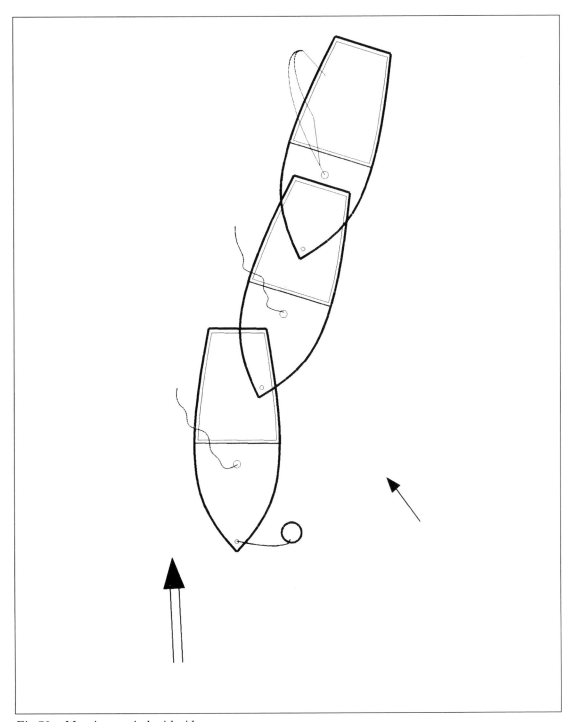

Fig 73   Mooring – wind with tide.

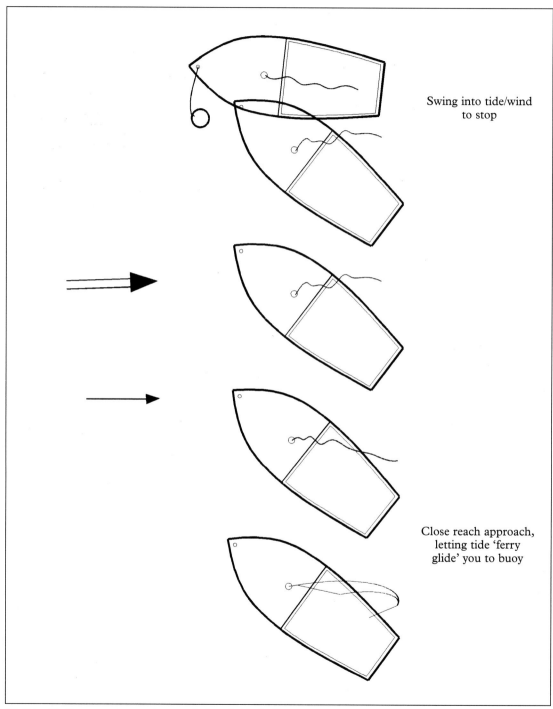

Swing into tide/wind
to stop

Close reach approach,
letting tide 'ferry
glide' you to buoy

Fig74   Sailing onto a mooring – wind and tide in line.

less the attitude that the yacht will lie once she is secure. Once again, a controlled close reach approach will be simplest and, if possible, will be even easier than when there is no tide since the tide will allow steerage-way to be maintained even when stationary relative to the buoy.

Unless the wind is angled at a perfect 60 degrees to the tide, it is likely that you will have to shoot into the wind a little in the final few metres to ensure that you are aiming virtually straight into the tide. Thus, in a wind-with-tide mooring, a combination of the two methods advocated for no-tide situations should be adopted.

If wind and tide are directly in line, it is possible to close reach towards the buoy, aiming at a point a little uptide of the buoy so that the tide drops you back. The buoy should be left to windward and the yacht turned into the tide at the last moment. If a shore transit is visible, this can be of great assistance in judging how much offset to allow for the tide.

Wind Against Tide
If the wind and tide are in direct opposition to each other (or nearly so), then the mainsail cannot be used for the approach because the yacht will be at least partly tide rode once secure and will thus be pointing downwind.

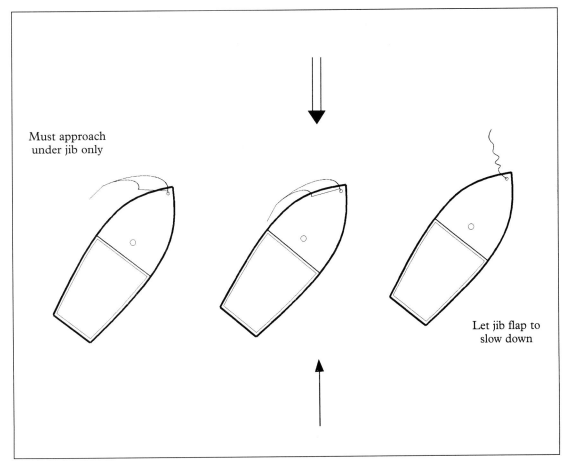

Must approach under jib only

Let jib flap to slow down

Fig 75 Sailing onto a mooring – wind against tide.

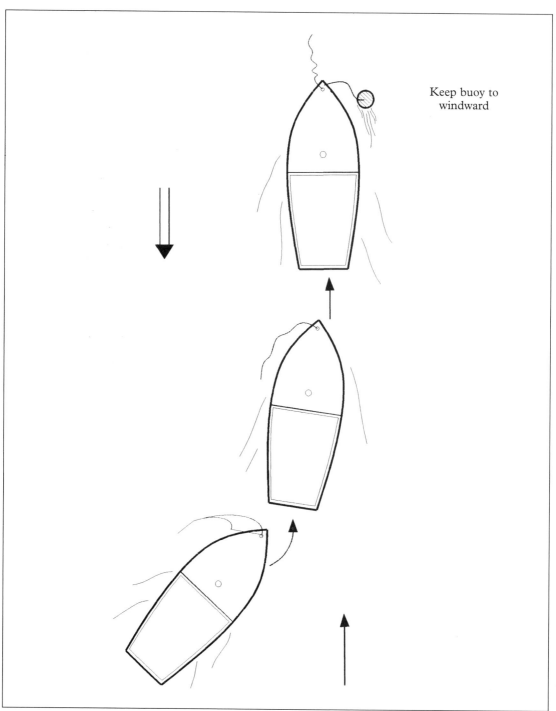

Keep buoy to
windward

Fig 76   Sailing onto a mooring – wind against tide – final approach.

Some skippers advocate a 'normal' mooring technique, shooting head-to-wind to pick the buoy up even when the tide is in opposition, then getting the mainsail down as soon as the buoy has been attached and before the yacht has swung to the tide.

There are two dangers inherent in this approach. Firstly, because you would be approaching the buoy downtide, your speed over the ground would be significantly higher than one would like, putting more pressure on the crew and more loads on cleats and ground tackle. Secondly, in my experience, this is the sort of occasion when the main halyard is going to jam, probably with the mainsail partially lowered – the resulting standing gybes are great fun for spectators to watch but not so much fun for those on the yacht!

So, having discussed the possibility of keeping the mainsail up for a wind-against-tide approach to a mooring, let us now forget it and concentrate on the more sensible and seamanlike way to execute the manoeuvre.

As already stated, the mainsail is bound to fill once you have secured to a wind-against-tide mooring and so it needs to be dropped before you make your final approach. This means that you will normally get into a position upwind and downtide of the mooring to carry this out, which will then allow you to run in towards the buoy against the tide. However if the tide is very strong and the wind light, it might be better to drop the mainsail in a position across the tide so that you can broad reach to the buoy making better speed.

However you decide to make your initial approach, the final boat length or two is nearly always best done straight into the tide since this lines you up well and means less last minute course adjustments will be needed.

As in wind-with-tide moorings, the buoy should be left on the side that allows you to sail straight past if you are going too fast, without danger of the buoy going underneath the yacht. This means that if the wind is

blowing from slightly to one side of the tidal flow, the buoy should be placed on your windward side. If the wind and tide are directly in line, either side will do equally well. In this case, since you will be running dead square into the buoy, it is easiest to put the buoy on the opposite side to the headsail since this makes life simpler for the foredeck crew.

The neatest and often safest way to finish the approach is to get rid of the headsail just before you reach the buoy, either furling it up if you have furling gear or dropping it on the deck if not. You can also use a progressive dropping or furling in the last few boat lengths to the buoy as a kind of decelerator, rather than just letting the sheet fly.

If you do not have headsail furling, you will need one person lowering the halyard and another crew member pulling the sail down and 'sheeting' it by holding the leech back and down. With the sail completely down or furled at the buoy there will be no flapping around the heads of the foredeck crew. You will also have reduced speed as much as is reasonably possible.

Should you need to go around again it will be an easy matter to rehoist or unfurl the headsail to regain speed. In any case you should still have steerage-way at the buoy since you will need to be stemming the tide.

Actually picking the buoy up is exactly the same as for any other type of swinging mooring.

Wind Across Tide

If you judge that the wind is blowing across the tidal stream then your approach will need to be on a reach. If the wind will be well forward of the beam when you are secured then you can treat it as if the wind and tide were together. However, if there is any risk that the mainsail will even partially fill when you are secured, then the approach must be made with just a headsail.

Once again, the best approach is almost

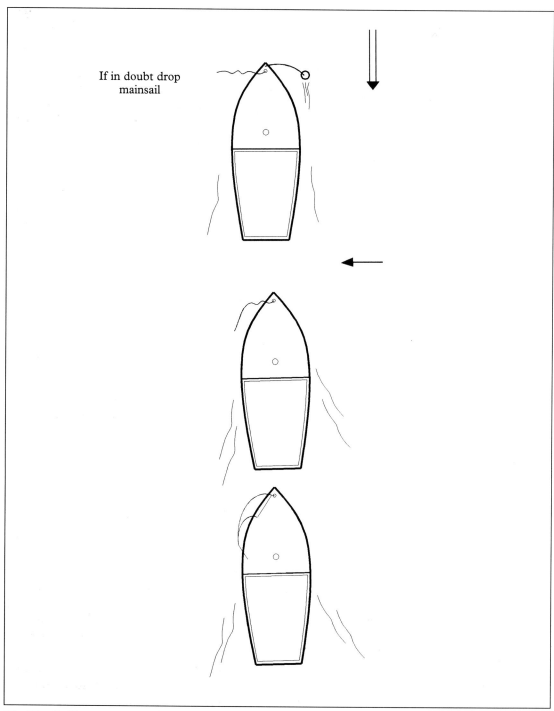

If in doubt drop
mainsail

Fig 77   *Sailing onto a mooring – wind across tide.*

certainly going to be straight into the tide which will determine which tack you will be on and which side to pick the buoy up on (windward as usual). The main difference between this and a wind-against-tide situation is that in most cases you will need to leave the headsail up until after you have secured to the buoy since not many yachts will reach well with a half lowered sail.

A controlled reach approach, spilling wind and slowing down as needed by releasing the sheet on the headsail is what is wanted. Once the buoy has been secured, the jib should be dropped in reasonably quick time to prevent it flapping itself to pieces for any longer than necessary.

Sailing Off a Mooring

Sailing off a mooring is the reverse of sailing onto it so far as your choice of sails is concerned. If you are lying head-to-wind or

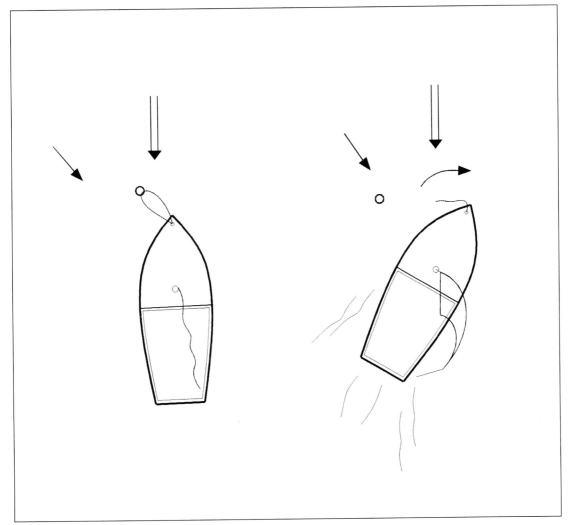

Fig 78   Sailing away under mainsail.

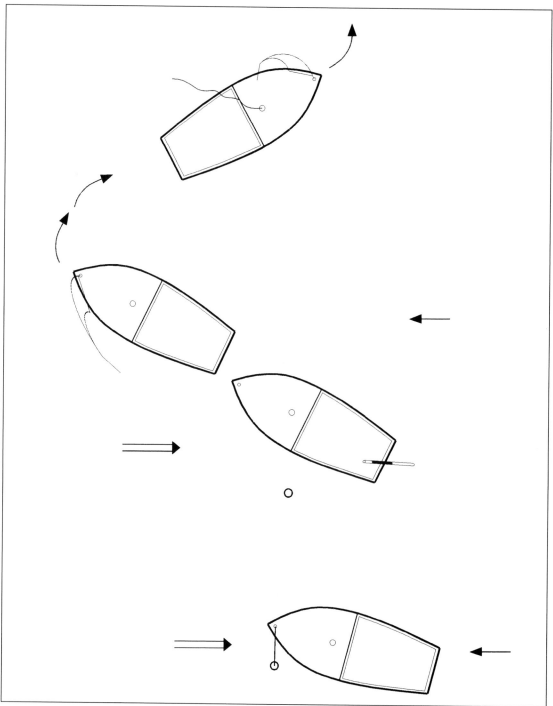

Fig 79   Slipping under bare poles.

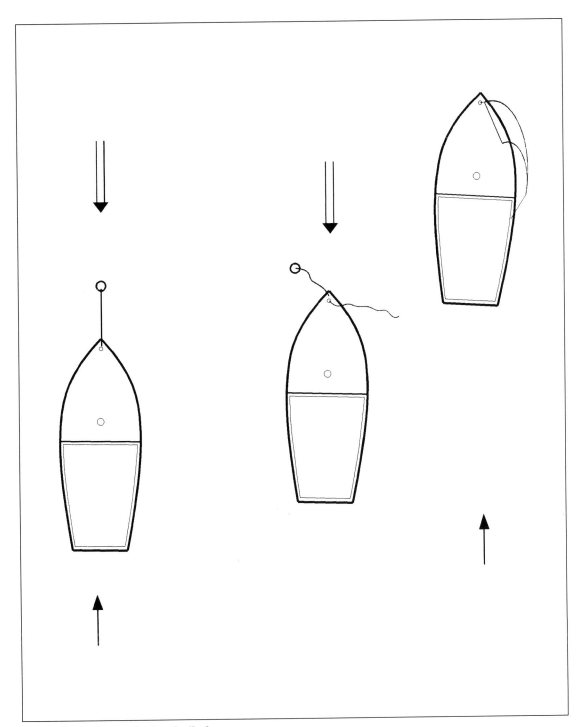

Fig 80   Slipping under headsail alone.

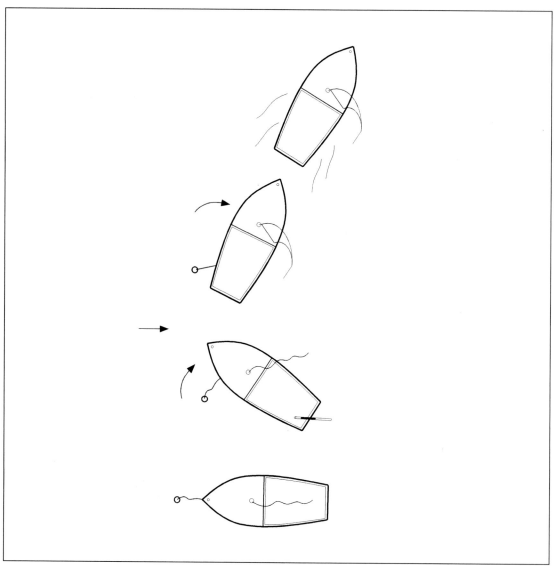

Fig 81   Using the buoy line as a pivot.

nearly so, then it is by far easier to sail away with just the mainsail, hoisting the jib once you are clear and any warps and/or mess on the foredeck has been tidied away.

If on the other hand, the wind is on or aft of the beam then the mainsail would not flap and cannot therefore be hoisted until you have left the mooring. In this case you will need to leave either under bare poles, hoisting the jib as soon as you have cleared the buoy or with the headsail hoisted before you slip.

In general terms, use the bare poles technique if the wind is strong and you do not have to manoeuvre too soon after relinquishing the mooring. Only have the headsail up before you slip if the wind is light or you might have to alter course quickly away from a dead run.

In either case, ensure that the buoy is going to be clear before slipping the mooring, if necessary using the action of the tide on the rudder to shear the yacht so that the buoy is to windward. Normally, the crew can just hold onto the slip line as you start to build up speed and let go as soon as it becomes slack. However, if you need to make a rapid alteration of course, it is often easiest to do this if the crew walk the mooring line down the windward side of the yacht as you build up speed. If it is then held firmly aft of amidships, it will give a good turning pivot for the yacht as you swing the helm over.

If the wind and tide were against each other so that you had to depart under headsail alone, getting the mainsail hoisted is the next priority. For this you need a remarkable amount of sea room where it is possible to sail with the wind well forward of the beam to allow the sail to flap as it is hoisted.

ANCHORING

Sailing to an Anchorage

In essence, sailing to an anchorage is almost identical to sailing onto a swinging mooring except that you do not need to be quite so precise in the positioning of the yacht. Certainly the same rules apply as to whether to use the mainsail or jib – that is, if the mainsail will definitely flap once anchored then use it, if in doubt take it down and use the headsail.

The anchor needs to be prepared so that it can be lowered without damage to the topsides and the correct amount of chain and/or warp should be flaked on the foredeck. As a general guide, use a length three times the expected depth of water if using all chain and

at least four and probably five times the depth if using mainly warp.

If anchoring in a place where there might be obstructions on the seabed or where it is rocky, there will be the danger of the anchor getting caught and being hard or impossible to raise when you want to leave. In this case, a trip line attached to the crown of the anchor can be invaluable.

How crowded the anchorage is will determine the type of trip line used. The simplest is to have a length of lightish rope maybe half as long again as the maximum depth, with a fender attached to its end. An alternative is to use a light, floating line, once again from the crown but this time brought back on board, ensuring that it is long enough not to trip the anchor until needed.

Approach the anchorage in the same way as if you were coming onto a mooring buoy and have the crew ready to let the anchor go. Then, as you reach your chosen spot, take all way off the yacht. If possible make her go astern, either by backing the mainsail, if wind and tide are together, or by dropping the headsail and letting the tide carry her back if under jib. Watch the shore or a nearby yacht abeam of your yacht to check the direction you are travelling in.

The anchor should be dropped as soon as the yacht has stopped making way forward. Your crew can then pay out enough cable so that the anchor reaches the bottom. Do not let all the cable go at once or it is likely to end up in a heap over the anchor, instead pay out the cable as the yacht drifts back away from the anchor.

Unless you are able to make a good sternboard or the tide is strong, it is unlikely that the anchor will bite in very well and it is often worth having the engine going for a few seconds in astern to get the anchor dug well into the seabed. You can usually feel if the anchor is dragging by holding the cable as it comes into the yacht – if the anchor is holding

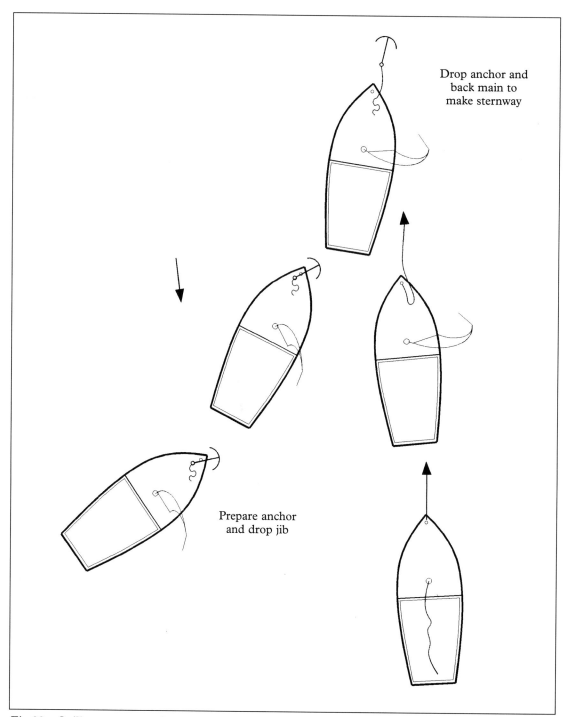

Drop anchor and
back main to
make sternway

Prepare anchor
and drop jib

Fig 82   Sailing onto an anchorage – no tide.

the cable will feel taut, if dragging you will feel the vibrations as the anchor bounces over the bottom.

Once you are happy that the anchor has bitten properly, try to take some shore transits so that you can check later to see if you have moved at all. At the same time, it is wise to hoist an anchor ball near the bow or to turn on an all round white anchor light to let other yachts know that you are anchored. Similarly, if you are using a trip line with a fender attached, it is well worth writing the yacht's name and 'anchor' on the fender so that other yachts do not think of it as a mooring buoy!

Sailing Away from an Anchorage

If wind and tide are both slack then it is usually possible simply to put the appropriate sail up, leave it flapping and pull the yacht manually to the anchor. It is then easy to raise the anchor and sail off. Sometimes though, either the anchor is so well dug into the seabed that your crew cannot get it to break out or the wind and/or tide are holding the yacht back from the anchor so hard that it is difficult to pull her up to the anchor.

In either of these cases it is often easiest to use the engine to motor up to the anchor, take a turn of the cable to hold it temporarily and then motor over the anchor with the cable virtually straight up and down. The power of the engine is thus utilized to break the anchor out. However, there will be times when for various reasons you do not want to or cannot use the engine and at these times you need to sail the anchor out.

If the wind and tide are in opposition, life is very simple. Hoist the headsail, sheet-in and sail towards the anchor in exactly the same way as if you were using the engine, pulling in the slack on the cable as you go. When directly above the anchor, once again take a turn and let the momentum of the yacht break the anchor out.

If lying head-to-wind the above will obviously not be possible since you will not be able to sail directly towards the anchor. Here, you need to hoist the mainsail and possibly the jib as well, back the jib to force the yacht onto one tack, towards the danger if there is one and sail close-hauled away from the anchor, without trying to pull in the cable.

Once you reach the extent of the anchor cable, at right angles to the anchor, go about as rapidly as possible. If you are a little lucky, you will now be able to sail on the opposite tack straight towards the anchor, and away from any danger, breaking the anchor out as before once you get the anchor cable up short.

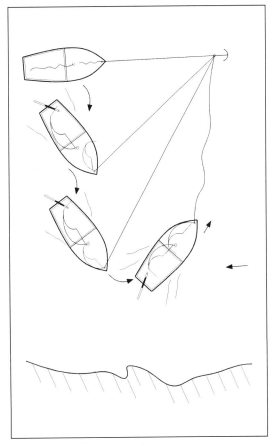

Fig 83   Tacking an anchor out.

PILE MOORINGS

Sailing onto Pile Moorings

We have already looked in some detail at pile moorings under power and most of what was discussed there still holds true.

In general terms, if wind and tide are together, then it is nearly always simplest to pick up the upstream, upwind pile as if it were a swinging mooring buoy, drop the mainsail and allow the yacht to drift back to the other pile. The tide can be used to shear the yacht if this is needed to counteract a slight offset of the wind.

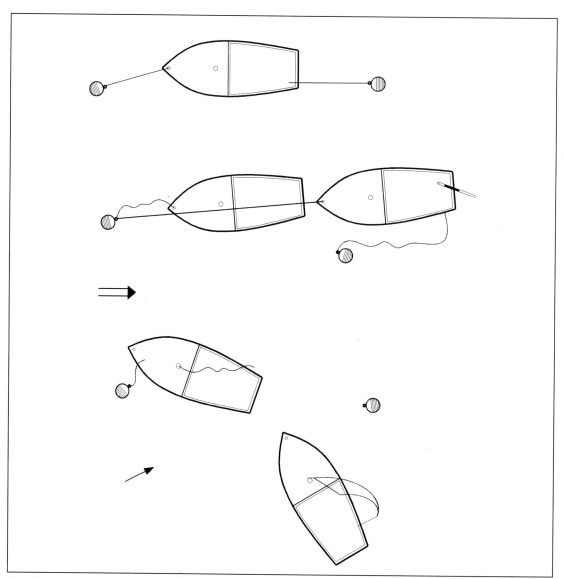

Fig 84   Pile moorings – wind with tide.

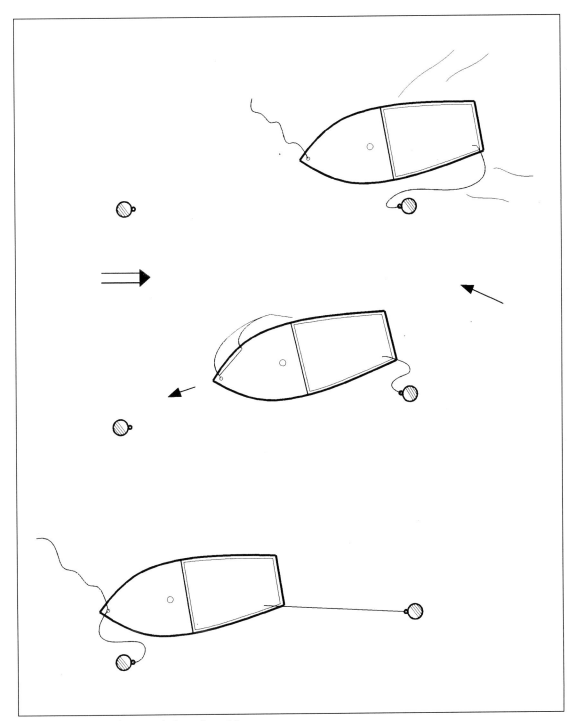

Fig 85   Pile moorings – wind against tide.

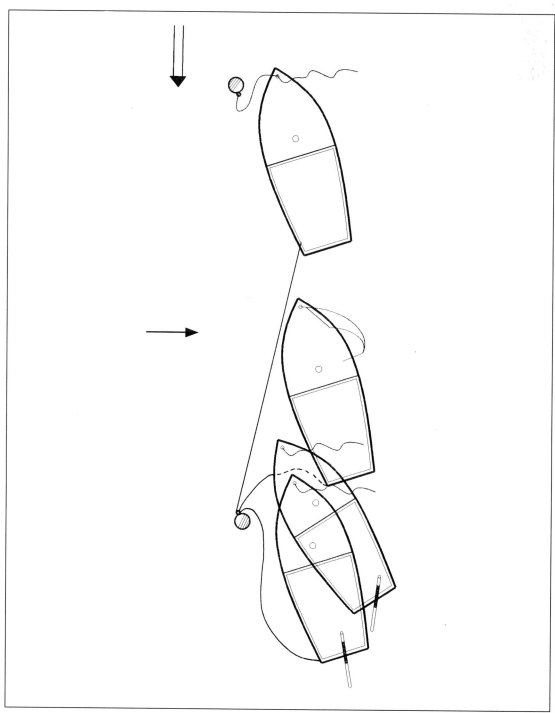

Fig 86   Pile moorings – close reach.

As with a mooring, ensure that the pile is positioned on the windward side of the yacht so that, in the event of an overshoot, you do not end up with the pile scratching the topsides. Never attempt to pick the pile up at the stem – a tiny error in boat-speed will always result in damage. Instead, aim to place the pile about a third of the way along the foredeck where it can be easily reached and where there is space for one crew member to hold it while another fastens the mooring line.

If the wind is either across or against the tide then there is no reason not to do a running moor. As with swinging moorings, whether the mainsail or headsail is used will depend on your confidence about the mainsail flapping. If unsure always use just the headsail.

In the same way as you would if under power, approach the first, downtide pile with it on your windward side and aim to slow right down with it just forward of amidships. Attach the long stern line and sheet-in again to sail up to the second pile.

If the direction between the piles is a close reach, the bow will almost certainly try to pay off as you sheet in and begin to regain speed. Because you know that this is going to happen, it is possible to counteract the effect by shearing the bow slightly to windward while the aft pile is being held, just before you sheet-in.

When the forward, upstream pile is reached, place it once again alongside halfway down the foredeck, attach the bow line and then drop or pull back until central between the piles.

Sailing Off Pile Moorings

Only ever attempt to sail off a pile mooring when heading into the current (if there is any). Attempting to sail off downtide is fraught with danger since there is a good chance you will hit the downstream pile before you have enough steerage-way to enable you to avoid it. Therefore, if you are going to sail off and are

pointing downtide, the first thing you will need to do is to swing the yacht around (covered elsewhere – see 'swinging ship').

Wind and Tide Together
If wind and tide are together then you will be able to sail off using the mainsail. First drop back to the stern pile and attach a long slip-rope, then pull up to the bow pile and do likewise. It will be best if you shorten the bow line so that you are quite close to the bow pile (but not so close that you are going to hit it). In most situations, you will be able to cast off the stern line allowing the yacht to lie from just the bow pile while you get the mainsail up, then sail off as if it were a swinging mooring. Occasionally, there will be other yachts or obstructions too near to allow your yacht to swing around, in which case you will need to keep hold of the stern line until moments before you slip the bow line.

As with a swinging mooring, it helps your manoeuvrability a lot if the member of crew slipping the bow line, holds onto the line and walks aft with it until the yacht has borne away far enough for the mainsail to set properly.

Wind and Tide Against Each Other
Here you will be sailing off into the current but downwind. Once again, rig slip-ropes at bow and stern but this time shorten up the stern line a little so that you are closer to the stern pile than to the one at the bow.

Get the genoa ready for hoisting or unfurling and when ready, hoist it but leave it flapping until it is properly up. As you sheet in, you should be able to let go of the bow line. The stern line will then act as a pivot enabling you to point the yacht safely into the channel, then and only then release the stern line and sail away.

Get well clear of other yachts before hoisting the mainsail since you will need to round up into the wind to do this and may need considerable space.

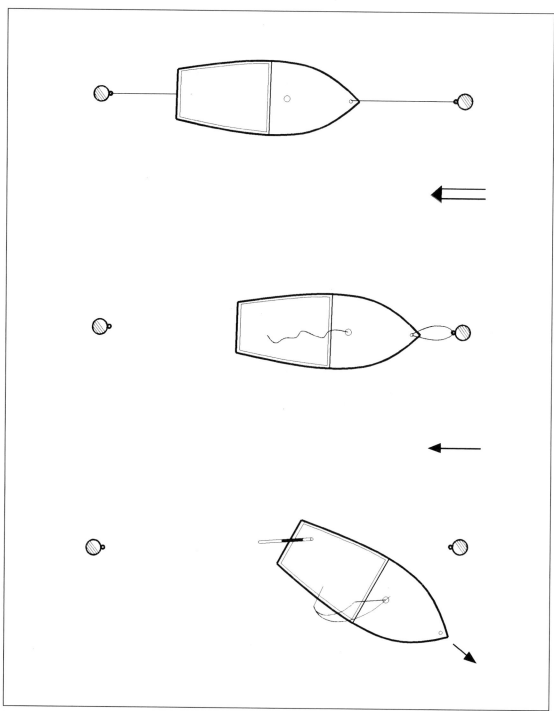

Fig 87   Sailing off piles – wind and tide together

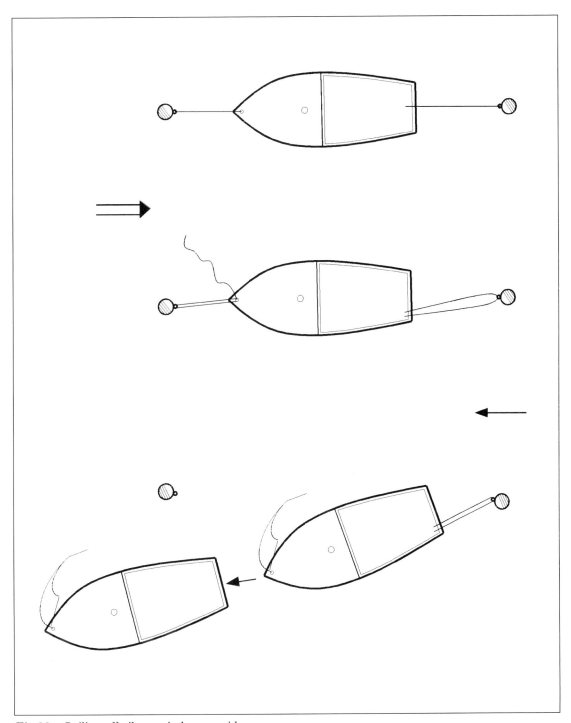

Fig 88   Sailing off piles – wind versus tide.

Wind Across Tide

As with any other mooring situation under sail, you need to consider whether the mainsail will flap if it is hoisted, before deciding how to deal with sailing off piles in a wind-across-tide scenario. If you either know that the mainsail will fill even when let right out or you are not quite sure, it is always safest to leave with only the genoa hoisted.

There are two different methods that can be used in this case. Which is chosen will depend on both the characteristics of the yacht

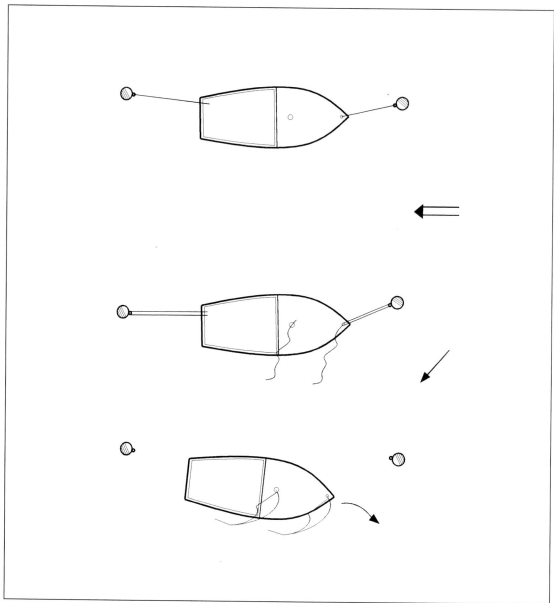

Fig 89 Sailing off piles – wind across tide – method one.

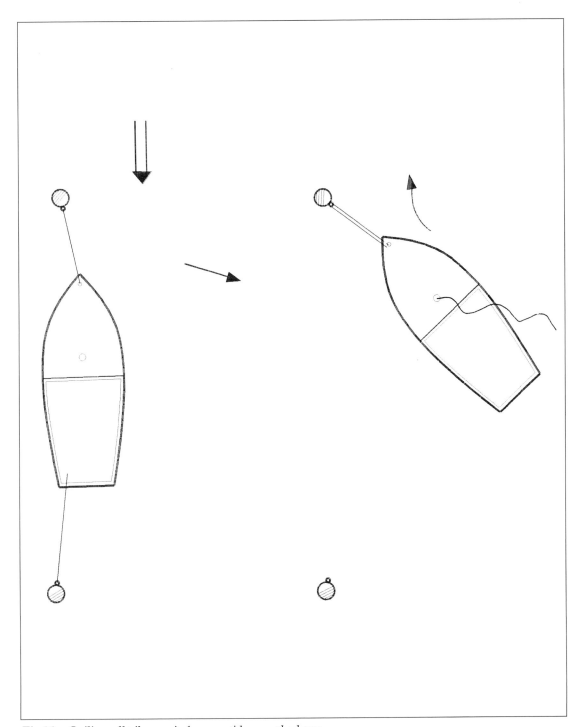

Fig 90   Sailing off piles – wind across tide – method two.

and on the amount of swinging room around the upstream pile.

The more normal method is effectively the same as for sailing off piles with the wind against tide, as in the previous section. Assuming that the tide is flowing up and down the line of the piles and the wind is blowing across the line, the first thing you must do is to ensure you are facing into the tide because, as before, leaving downtide carries too many risks to be worth attempting. The only case where this will not be true is when there is a strongish breeze and weak tide. You might then be confident of being blown away from danger and getting adequate steerage-way in a reasonable time, even if pointing downtide. Therefore, if facing downtide, it will be normal to swing your yacht around using the techniques already described earlier.

Having got the yacht facing the right way, next look at the wind direction and if it is from anywhere near or aft of the beam, make the decision to leave under headsail alone. If the wind is coming from well forward of the beam then it will be quite safe and in fact easier to use the mainsail for your departure.

Get both bow and stern lines organised as slip-ropes and remove all other mooring lines. Hoist the appropriate sail with it flapping, then sheet-in and at the same time cast off the slip-ropes. It is usually best to cast off both bow and stern lines at virtually the same time if possible; otherwise the bow line should be let go before the stern line so that the bow will pay off away from the pile and wind.

Always sail off to leeward of the piles since the yacht is bound to make considerable leeway until she has built up speed and it may be hard to get to windward of the bow pile.

If the tide is not very strong and/or you feel that your yacht will not sail well without the mainsail but you are lying with the wind too far astern to risk hoisting it, then a second method may be used. As long as there is enough room to leeward of the upstream pile

for the yacht to swing around, you can slip the stern line completely before any sails are hoisted and lie to the upstream pile by your bow for a time, effectively as if it were a swinging mooring. Leaving is then the same as for a swinging moor in a wind-across-tide situation.

ALONGSIDE BERTHS

Sailing Onto Alongside Berths

Sailing onto alongside berths is a skill which is not often practised by the majority of yachtsmen. In some cases, attempting to sail into a tricky inside berth in a marina, where a mistake could cause untold damage to both your own and other yachts, is just not worth the risk unless you and your crew are very sure of your abilities. There are however, a great number of situations where sailing alongside is not really any more difficult than motoring into the berth and where there would be a way out if a mistake were to be made. Most importantly, there is the odd occasion when the engine has broken down or you have run out of fuel and need to sail in. A lot of skippers would not feel confident in doing this and should really have practised the manoeuvre in simple situations before it became a necessity.

If sailing onto a berth for fun or practice, it is nearly always a good idea to have your engine running in neutral since this can give you a safety net if it is needed.

The main things to remember are, firstly that it is always easiest to head into the tide if this is possible. You should always be putting the yacht alongside, never (except in rare circumstances) putting the bow onto the pontoon or quay since this latter move involves extremely fine judgement of distance and speed and a tiny mistake can leave you hitting the berth head on with considerable force.

Lastly as with any other berthing situation, you should have thought about what might go wrong, if, for example, the wind changes at the last moment. It is always best to have planned some alternatives and a way to 'bale out' if it does go wrong.

Certainly when practising sailing alongside, try to pick a berth which is well within your capabilities. You can then move to your allocated berth later, under power or by warping if necessary.

In anything other than very small yachts, sailing alongside will always be easier and safer if you think and plan ahead well. Fenders need to be ready and at the right height for the berth you are going to use, mooring lines and the crew to tend them need to be sorted well in advance and the choice of sails and approach needs to be made early enough so that there is no last minute panic.

As with other moorings, it is usual to use the mainsail if confident that it will flap completely once alongside, otherwise drop the main before making your final approach and come in with just the headsail.

No Tide – Head-To-Wind

If the berth you are coming onto is an outside one with free direction of approach, this should present few greater difficulties than sailing up to a swinging mooring. If you have a choice of sides of the berth and the wind is not blowing quite up and down the line of the pontoon, choose the one where you will be blown off the pontoon if possible – so long as this allows you a safe route out if you are going too fast (or too slow). If you do have a choice of approach directions, choose the one which gives you the least possible angle to turn the yacht at the last moment, preferably such that you will not need to tack to come alongside.

The basic approach will be to get your warps and fenders ready and drop the headsail (unless the wind is very light) having first had

a passing look at the berth. Having looked at the berth, you should know what sort of cleats or bollards there are for tying up and can thus prepare the warps accordingly.

Once ready, approach the berth on a close reach, aiming about a boat length downwind from your intended stopping point and gradually slowing the boat down, as you get closer to the berth, by letting the mainsheet out. When just about dead downwind of the berth, turn the boat into the wind and towards the berth, letting the sail flap, steering alongside and, unless you have misjudged the amount of way the yacht carries, gliding to a halt alongside.

In this case, since there is no tide, the important lines will be the bow and stern ropes which can be used, if necessary, to surge the yacht to a halt. Once she is stationary, they should be used as breast ropes and a stern spring rigged as soon as possible to prevent the wind pushing the yacht backwards.

The only tricky part of this manoeuvre is judging how far downwind of the berth to be aiming on your approach and to get this right. You do need to have practised shooting head to wind in different wind strengths to see how fast your yacht will slow down.

In most situations, it will be better to approach too slowly and not quite make the berth, rather than approaching too fast and overshooting at speed. Remember however, that once you have turned head-to-wind, pulling the sail in will not help you to get going again and if you do undershoot, you will have little option but to let the sail out, bear away and make a second complete approach.

If you are going too slowly and made your turn too far downwind from the berth so that you actually stop moving forward, the wind will blow the yacht backwards. You will need to make a sternboard, holding the main out to windward and steering as if in astern, until you are pointing far enough away from the wind for the sail to fill on the usual leeward side.

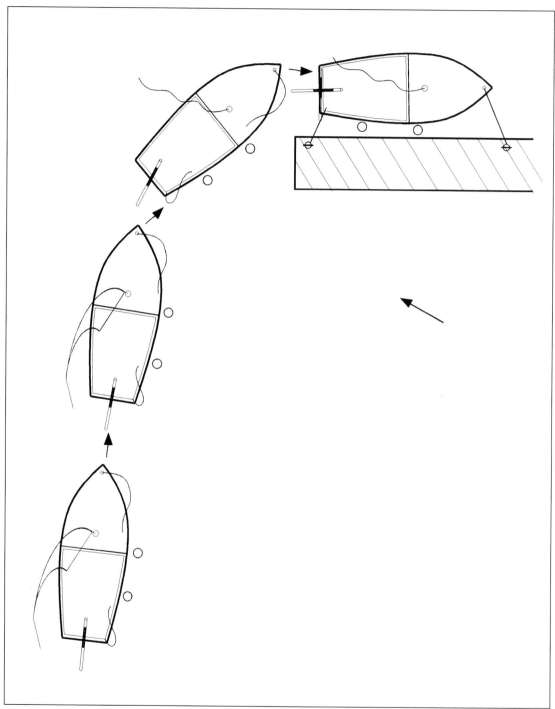

Fig 91   Sailing alongside – no tide.

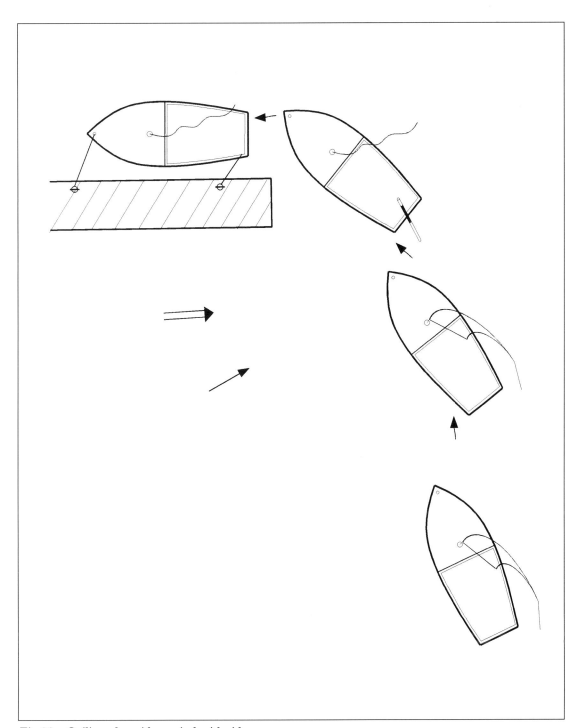

Fig 92   Sailing alongside – wind with tide.

Wind and Tide Together

This situation is essentially the same as berthing head-to-wind with no tide as described in the previous section but it is (or should be) just a little bit easier.

The only parts of the manoeuvre to change are the final approach on a close reach and exactly where to aim before turning into the wind. Because the tide will be setting you downwind, you will obviously need to be aiming slightly closer to the actual berth than if there was no tide and you will need to be correspondingly closer to the berth when you make your final turn.

Judging your approach across the tide is always a bit tricky and can be helped considerably by the use of transits – alter your reaching angle so that you track straight towards the point on the shore where you judge you will need to swing up into the wind.

Once alongside, both wind and tide will be pushing the yacht backwards and it will therefore be important to have a stern spring ready as one of the first lines ashore, together with a bow line.

Wind Across Tide – Windward Berth

Sailing onto a pontoon or other alongside berth when the tide is running up and down the berth and the wind is blowing you off should not be hard. The only real problem stems from the fact that, as you slow down to a stop to come alongside, the yacht is bound to make more and more leeway. This could, especially in strong winds, cause difficulties for the crew members taking the lines ashore.

Unless the wind is well forward of the beam and you are sure that the mainsail will flap, it is best to get rid of the mainsail before making your approach, then come alongside with just the headsail up. If you do decide to use the mainsail, ensure that the kicking strap (boom vang) is released completely otherwise the leech of the main is likely to drive you forward even with the sheet let right off.

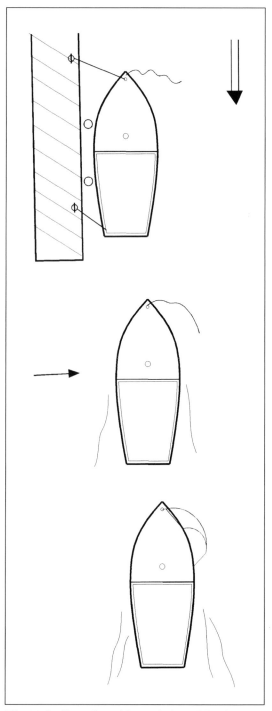

Fig 93 Sailing alongside – windward berth.

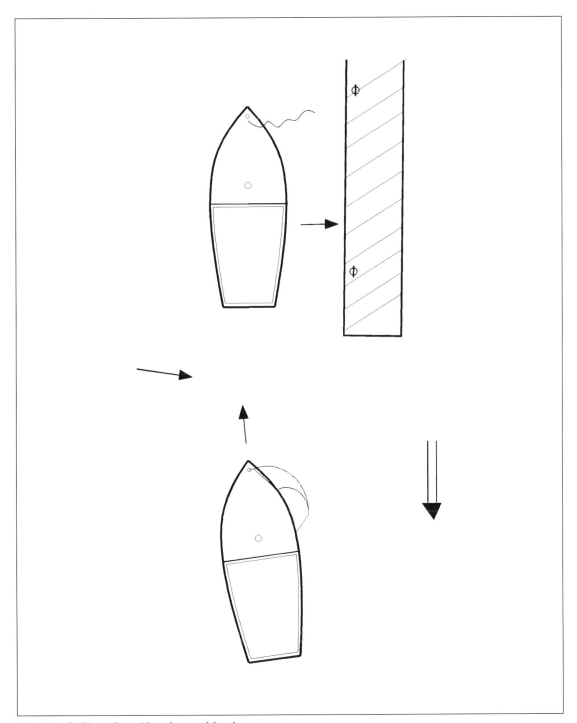

Fig 94   Sailing alongside – leeward berth.

Approach as near to straight into the tide and straight along the berth as possible to avoid the need for last minute alterations of course, when boat-speed will be at its minimum and manoeuvrability will be at its lowest. Let the sail out to reduce speed long before you get to the berth and then pull it in again to give a little more drive if necessary. Once alongside, let it flap completely before dropping it as quickly as possible.

In this case, with the wind blowing the yacht away from the pontoon it will be important to position the yacht really close alongside the berth to give the crew a fair chance of getting their lines ashore. If the wind is very strong and it looks as if you will be blown off too quickly to get the lines made fast, it can be worth either using a couple of bystanders to take the lines, or even dropping one or two of your crew off on a 'fly past' before making your real approach.

If you do use bystanders in this or any other mooring situation, make very sure that they are instructed exactly what is wanted of them. For example, 'please put the loop at the end of this rope over *that* bollard' or 'take a turn around *that* cleat with the end of the rope and let us do the pulling from on board'. Failure to give clear instructions will nearly always end with the wrong ropes being taken first and being put onto the wrong cleats!

Wind Across Tide – Leeward Berth

In essence it makes little difference whether the wind is blowing you onto or away from the pontoon. Obviously your crew are going to have an easier time getting the ropes ashore with the wind blowing you on but in most other respects the procedures are going to be the same as described in the previous section.

The main difficulty lies in the possibility of getting ropes, such as jib or mainsheet, caught on mooring cleats as you slide along the pontoon and you need to be very aware of this possibility. If coming alongside a wall which is

higher than your topsides or if there are piles sticking up above the line of the pontoons then you also have a real danger of ripping whichever sail is in use. Therefore if either of these situations prevail, it will actually be best to make the final few metres of your approach under bare poles, using the momentum of the yacht to get you onto the berth.

The other problem is with sailing off again if for any reason your approach is not quite right. With the wind blowing you onto a lee shore, it will not be easy to sail past and away unless you have quite a lot of steerage-way. If you do decide to sail on past the berth, there is an even greater risk of being arrested by a sheet caught on a cleat or of damaging the topsides if you end up too close to the berth. For all these reasons, you should aim to put the yacht about a metre off the pontoon, giving a bit of room for manoeuvre and leeway while still being close enough for crew members to get ashore.

Wind Against Tide

In a lot of ways this is the easiest time to sail alongside. You should always head into the tide otherwise there will be no way to stop the yacht and you should obviously only be using the headsail, having first taken down the main in a convenient position a little way upwind from the berth.

As with other sailing alongside situations, it is easiest to choose the side which will blow you away from the berth rather than onto it if this is feasible. However, in this case it does not matter too much since you will almost certainly end up under bare poles.

Prepare the fenders and warps as usual. This time you will definitely need both stern and bow lines as priorities but the spring should not be quite so vital as the wind and tide should cancel each out to some extent.

Position yourself upwind/downtide of the berth much as if you were going to pick up a swinging moor and take the mainsail down.

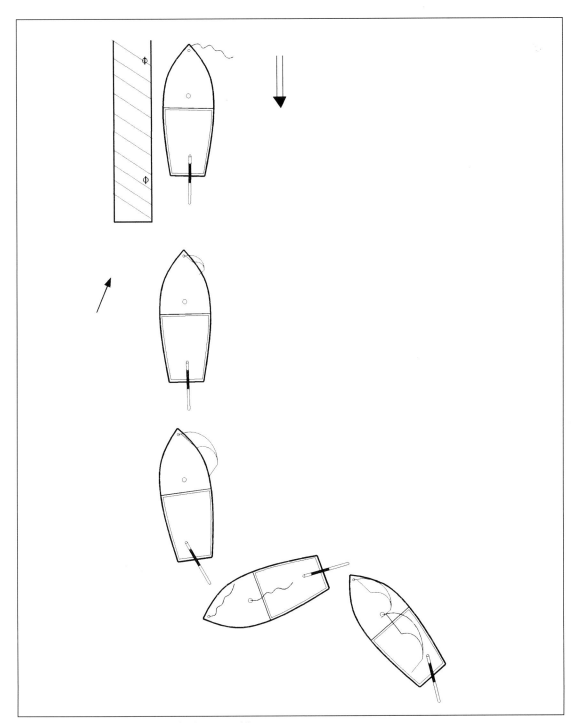

Fig 95   Sailing alongside – wind versus tide.

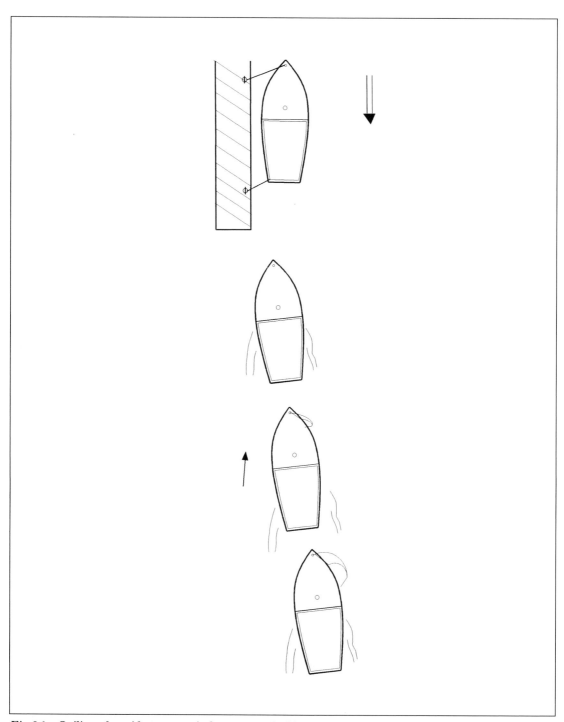

Fig 96   Sailing alongside, strong wind versus weak tide.

Having got the main down, sail against the tide towards the berth with just the headsail. You should reduce speed by either furling or partially dropping the headsail so that, when actually alongside you are just stemming the tide and are stationary over the land.

If the wind is quite strong and the tide weak, it may not be possible to slow down to this extent in which case you will need to get down to bare poles quite a distance from the berth to give as long as possible for the yacht to slow down.

If, even under bare poles, you are still travelling relatively fast when you arrive alongside, get lines from both the stern and bow lines onto shore cleats behind the intended position of the yacht and use these lines to act as brakes – surging them out to take way off the yacht in a controlled fashion. As soon as she has stopped, transfer them to the normal positions for use as breast lines.

Sailing Onto a Berth Where There is No Choice

Usually when coming into a marina, you will not be given much choice as to the berth you are going to use. Apart from the berths at the very end of the pontoons there is unlikely to be a way out if you are going too fast and in most cases very precise boat handling will be required.

Until you are confident with handling your boat under sail in very restricted situations, ignore the berth which has been allocated to you if you have to sail on, unless it is an easy one. Regardless of a little hassle later, it is always better to get safely onto an easy berth. You can then move the yacht once secure rather than attempting to sail onto a berth where you know your skills are being pushed to dangerous limits and you will probably end up damaging your own or someone else's yacht.

Never try to sail into a berth downtide since you will not have any effective brakes. Using springs to stop should only be a last ditch measure – if the crew does not get them on and surge them correctly you will either end up ploughing into the yacht in front or else ripping the cleats out of your deck.

If offered such a berth over the radio, explain your situation to the docking master and try to get him to offer you a berth where you will come in facing into the tide. If this is impossible, try to find a closely adjacent uptide berth as a temporary measure.

Sailing Off an Alongside Berth

It is generally easier to sail away from an alongside berth than it is to sail onto one because you can take your time to decide how best to perform the manoeuvre and it is usually simply a case of being well organised with no critical boat handling required.

As with most other situations, it is usually best to sail off facing into the tide (if any) since this will make it easier to build up a reasonable steerage-way before you are travelling too fast over the ground. Once again, choice of mainsail, headsail or both will depend firstly on whether the mainsail would flap as it is hoisted and secondly on wind strength.

If the wind is forward of the beam, it is possible to spring off in just the same way as you can when leaving under power. With the wind aft of the beam this is harder because there is no way to make the yacht go in reverse. However, if there is a reasonable strength of tide you can use this to spring the yacht off, hoisting the headsail once the yacht is pointing well out into the channel.

Wind With Tide

If wind and tide are both flowing down the pontoon or wall where you are berthed, the first thing to do is to make sure you are facing into the elements, if necessary swinging the yacht round using warps as described under 'Swinging Ship'.

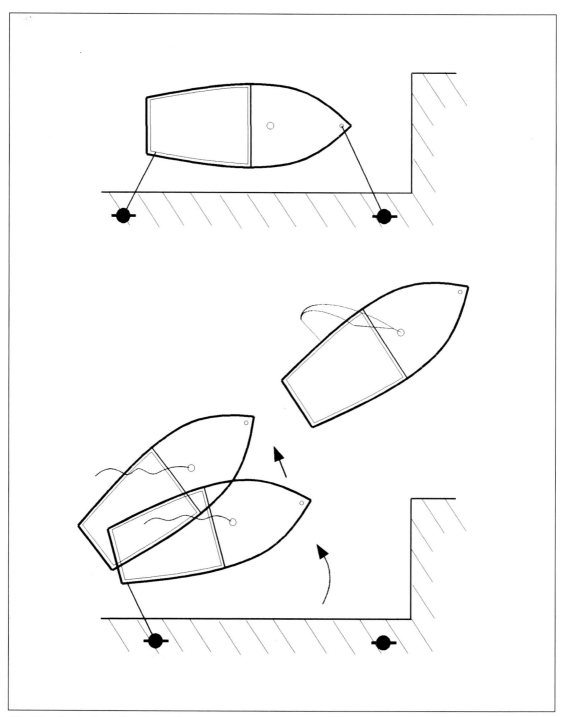

Fig 97   Springing off under sail.

Once facing the right way, get the warps organized with slip-ropes on bow and stern breast ropes and on the short stern spring. The latter will be needed to stop the yacht being forced backwards by wind and tide. Long head and stern ropes and the bow spring can be removed.

The next step is to get both mainsail and headsail ready for hoisting and to plan the manoeuvres which will be required once you

have slipped. It is important to decide whether you will need to go to windward or gybe around and to brief your crew appropriately.

Hoist the mainsail and get it set up with clew outhaul and halyard tension as required but with the kicking strap and sheet eased right out to allow the sail to flap.

Finally cast off the bow line followed by the stern line, leaving the short stern spring on until the yacht has borne away sufficiently for

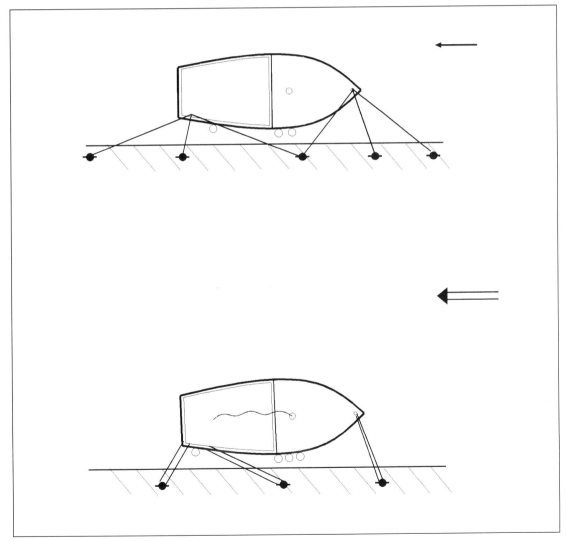

Fig 98   Preparing to sail off, wind with tide.

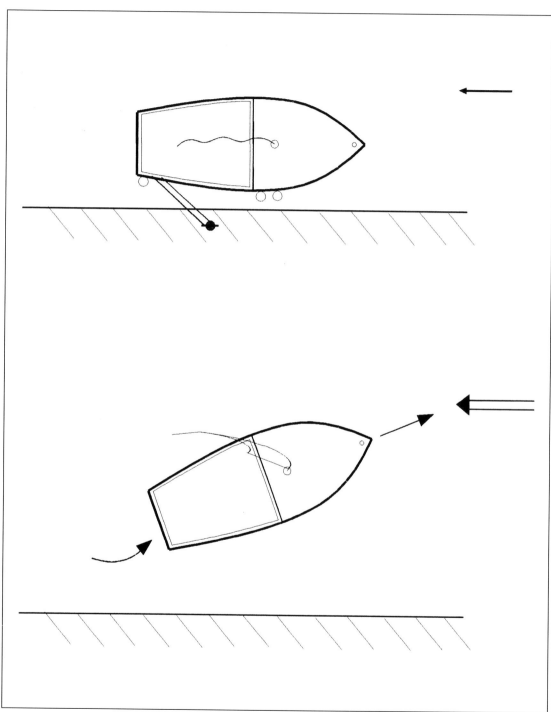

Fig 99   Sailing away from alongside, wind with tide.

the sail(s) to fill. Sheet in the mainsail and as the pressure comes off the spring, cast that off as well. Once clear, get the fenders inboard and hoist the headsail.

Wind Against Tide

If the wind and tide are in opposition then, as in other mooring situations, you will have little option but to leave under headsail alone. As always, make sure the yacht is facing into the tide unless the tide is very weak and the wind is strong, when it may be better to leave downtide.

Rig slip-ropes for both breast lines and a short central spring to stop the yacht surging up and down the berth before you are ready to leave.

Ensure that the headsail is ready to hoist or

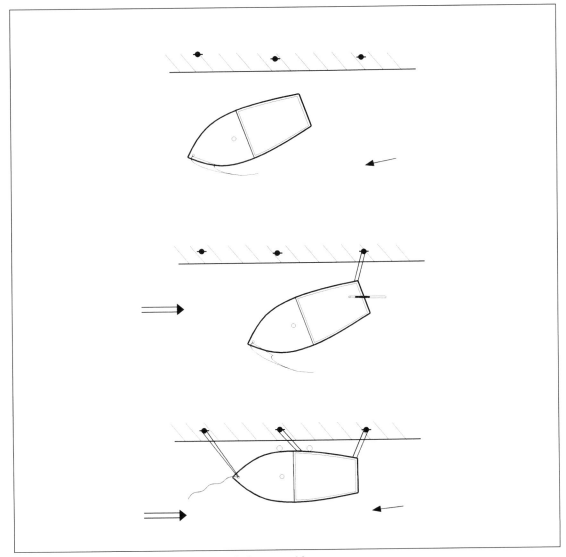

Fig 100 Sailing away from alongside, wind versus tide.

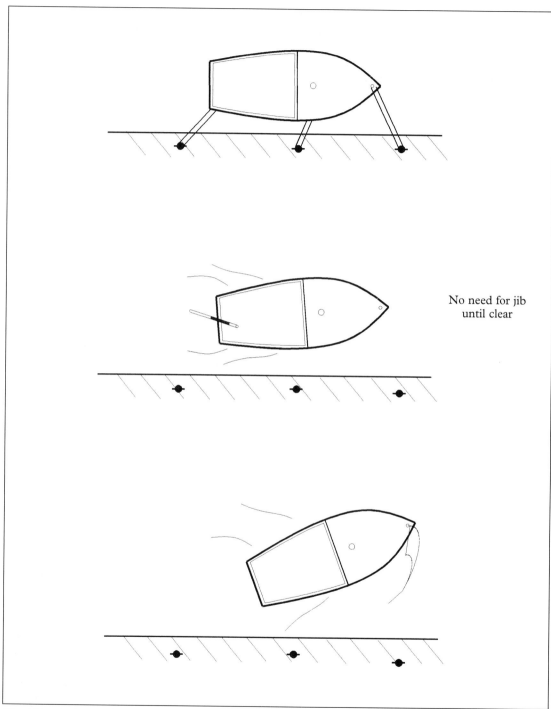

No need for jib
until clear

Fig 101   Sailing away from a leeward alongside mooring with wind with tide.

unfurl and that the sheets are not caught underneath fender lines or mooring warps. Hoist the headsail and sheet it in, then at more or less the same time, cast off the spring and bow line and use the stern line as a pivot to help steer the yacht away from the pontoon. As soon as you can see that you are able to sail in a straight line away from the berth, cast off the stern line and sail into clear water before hoisting the mainsail.

If the wind is very strong, it is often easier to delay hoisting the headsail until you are actually underway, relying on the windage of the hull and rig to give you enough initial driving power. This will be especially true if the wind is blowing you onto the berth as it is not advisable to have the headsail and its sheets flapping over the pontoon and of course over the crew members trying to cast off forward.

Wind Across Tide – Windward Berth

In some ways this is the easiest situation of all when sailing away from an alongside berth. With the wind coming across the yacht you will be able to reach away from the mooring, either with headsail if the wind is on a beam or broad reach or with the mainsail (and possibly headsail as well) if lying in a close reaching position. The wind will blow you away from the pontoon and there should be no danger of sails or ropes getting caught on shoreside obstructions.

Once again, make sure the yacht is facing into the tide, although this is one occasion when you might be able to get away with leaving downtide so long as there are no obstructions (other yachts for instance) immediately downtide of the berth. Rig slip lines for both breast ropes, a short central 'breast line' to stop the yacht surging up and down the berth and get the appropriate sail(s) ready for hoisting.

Hoist the sail(s), leaving them flapping until ready to slip and then slip first the central line

and the bow line followed shortly afterwards by the stern line. Allow the yacht to drift a metre or two away from the berth and then sheet in and sail away.

Wind Across Tide – Leeward Berth

This is the worst possible combination of wind and tide for sailing off. If the tide is strong and the wind is light, it may be possible to spring off far enough to allow you to sail off on a close reach. Even then there will always be the danger of being blown straight back onto the berth as soon as the lines have been released. If you are on a lee berth and must sail off, the best way in a lot of situations will be to take warps to a windward berth and warp yourself upwind, then sail off with ease.

If there is no other convenient berth to windward, it may be necessary to row an anchor up to windward, drop that and winch yourself up to the anchor to get away from the lee shore. If doing this, it is always best to put the anchor and all the anchor cable in the dinghy (use the kedge line with mainly warp and just a little bit of chain), row up to where you want the anchor positioned and lower the anchor over the side. Once the anchor is on the bottom, drift back down to the yacht, paying out the anchor cable as you go. In my experience trying to do it the other way, rowing upwind with the anchor cable attached to the yacht and dragging out behind the dinghy, is almost impossible. It is still very difficult even if you have an outboard engine.

If you are planning to use an anchor to help you off the lee shore, it will be necessary to take it quite a long way to windward, at least four or five boat lengths, otherwise you will end up too close to the lee shore to make sailing off a safe option.

Obviously, if the wind is very light and especially if you are dealing with quite a small yacht, the problems are not nearly so great and it may be possible to hoist the sails and push or spring her off sufficiently to get the sails

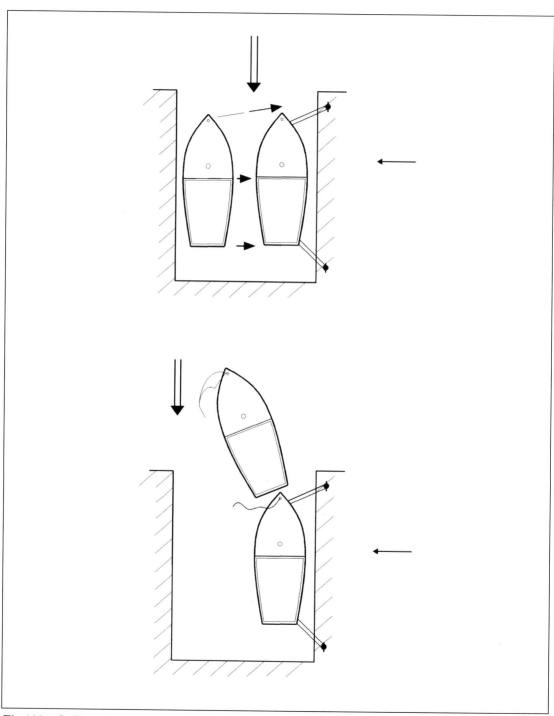

Fig 102   Sailing off – worst situation.

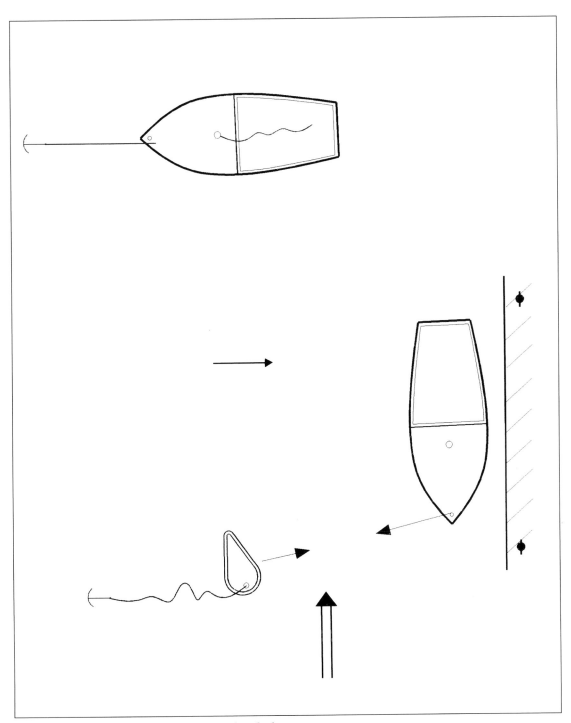

Fig 103   Rowing an anchor to windward as kedge.

filled and way on her. In general however, do not underestimate the difficulties associated with sailing a cruiser off a lee shore type of berth and if you have any choice in the matter, do not allow yourself to get caught in this situation!

INDEX